Cambridge Elements

Elements in Women Theatre Makers
edited by
Elaine Aston
Lancaster University
Melissa Sihra
Trinity College Dublin

PERFORMING FEMALE INTIMACY IN JAPAN'S TAKARAZUKA REVUE

Nobuko Anan
Kansai University

Shaftesbury Road, Cambridge CB2 8EA, United Kingdom

One Liberty Plaza, 20th Floor, New York, NY 10006, USA

477 Williamstown Road, Port Melbourne, VIC 3207, Australia

314–321, 3rd Floor, Plot 3, Splendor Forum, Jasola District Centre, New Delhi – 110025, India

103 Penang Road, #05–06/07, Visioncrest Commercial, Singapore 238467

Cambridge University Press is part of Cambridge University Press & Assessment, a department of the University of Cambridge.

We share the University's mission to contribute to society through the pursuit of education, learning and research at the highest international levels of excellence.

www.cambridge.org
Information on this title: www.cambridge.org/9781009554978

DOI: 10.1017/9781009555012

© Nobuko Anan 2025

This publication is in copyright. Subject to statutory exception and to the provisions of relevant collective licensing agreements, no reproduction of any part may take place without the written permission of Cambridge University Press & Assessment.

When citing this work, please include a reference to the DOI 10.1017/9781009555012

First published 2025

A catalogue record for this publication is available from the British Library

ISBN 978-1-009-55497-8 Hardback
ISBN 978-1-009-55498-5 Paperback
ISSN 2634-2391 (online)
ISSN 2634-2383 (print)

Cambridge University Press & Assessment has no responsibility for the persistence or accuracy of URLs for external or third-party internet websites referred to in this publication and does not guarantee that any content on such websites is, or will remain, accurate or appropriate.

For EU product safety concerns, contact us at Calle de José Abascal, 56, 1°, 28003 Madrid, Spain, or email eugpsr@cambridge.org

Performing Female Intimacy in Japan's Takarazuka Revue

Elements in Women Theatre Makers

DOI: 10.1017/9781009555012
First published online: July 2025

Nobuko Anan
Kansai University
Author for correspondence: Nobuko Anan, n.anan@kansai-u.ac.jp

Abstract: Japan's Takarazuka Revue is arguably the most commercially successful all-female theatre company in the world. Renowned for its glamour-laden staging of musicals and revues, the company's signature shows are heterosexual Western romances where women play both male and female roles. Since its audience consists almost entirely of women, Takarazuka creates a space for queer intimacy between performers and ardent female fans. This Element analyses the recent experimental show, *The Poe Clan*, directed by Koike Shūichirō, which portrays a male homoerotic relationship, argued as a façade for a queer, kin-like relationship between women. It also explores works by the female director Ueda Kumiko, which depict an anti-capitalist shared commons for female intimacy. These shows exhibit resistant girls' aesthetics, expressed in the company's two-dimensional performance style.

Keywords: Takarazuka Revue, Japanese theatre, queer, lesbian, manga

© Nobuko Anan 2025

ISBNs: 9781009554978 (HB), 9781009554985 (PB), 9781009555012 (OC)
ISSNs: 2634-2391 (online), 2634-2383 (print)

Contents

1 Gender and Sexual Conundrum of the Takarazuka Revue   1

2 Female Queer Kinship and *The Poe Clan*   12

3 Ueda Kumiko's Experiments: De-capitalizing TAKARAZUKA   27

   Postscript   50

   References   53

1 Gender and Sexual Conundrum of the Takarazuka Revue

Foreign visitors to Kobe, Osaka, and Kyoto may be struck by the sight of posters in trains and at train stations of two women, one dressed as a man, depicted in romantic poses such as hugging, touching, and almost kissing (see Figure 1). These posters advertise musicals and revues of the Takarazuka Revue Company (Takarazuka kagekidan), which is an offshoot of the Hankyu Railway (Hankyū dentetsu). It advertises these shows throughout its train network between Kobe and Kyoto, as well as in its associated Hankyu department stores. The reason only women appear in these advertisements is because the Takarazuka Revue is an all-female company where women play both male and female characters in romantic love stories.

Takarazuka attracts predominantly female spectators: the audience is more than 80 per cent women (The Takarazuka Revue 2022: 2), thus rendering male spectators marginal to what feels like an only-female space.[1] The company's shows are enormously popular: its theatres are large (Takarazuka Grand Theater 2,550 seats; Bow Hall 526 seats; Tokyo Takarazuka Theater 2,069 seats), and tickets are almost always sold out. There are more than 1,400 performances each year (Azuma 2015: 74), and the annual audience attendance reached a record 3.1 million in 2018 (Hankyu Hanshin Holdings 2023: 64). As of 2010, the company boasted that it occupied 10 per cent of the theatre market in Japan (Hankyu Hanshin Holdings 2010: 41). To support this vast audience, the company has five troupes, each of which has about eighty performers, and they perform not only in the company's theatres but also in various venues around Japan and abroad. Ticket prices are from JPY 3,500 to 12,500 (GBP 18 to 66 as of December 2024), and audience members appear to be at least middle class and financially secure. All told, Takarazuka is a seriously big business and arguably the most commercially successful all-female theatre company in the world.

For a Western audience, an all-female company staging romances might appear to have a niche lesbian identity, but on the contrary, this is a mainstream commercial company that promotes itself as 'healthy' (*kenzen na*) entertainment for everyone regardless of gender and age (The Takarazuka Revue 2022: 2, 4).[2] Although its over-the-top performances with flashy, gaudy costumes may also

---

[1] To be precise, this is the percentage of female members signed up to the official fan club. However, the fan club is essentially the same as the entire audience because tickets are sold first to members in the fan club and only a limited number of tickets is offered to the general public.
[2] Unless otherwise stated, I have translated Japanese quotations into English. For the titles of Takarazuka productions, I cite the official English translations. However, occasionally I have modified the wording of a title if awkwardly expressed. Also note that I follow the Japanese name order where a family name comes before a given name except when authors publish in English.

Figure 1 Poster of a production, *Moonlight over the Sea at Nigitatsu* (*Nigitatsu no umi ni tsuki izu*) (2025), by the Star Troupe of the Takarazuka Revue hanging in a Hankyu train (photo taken by the author).

invoke campy, queer sensibilities, the company treats its productions as conventional and innocent romances, like the older love stories of Disney that are popular among Japanese women. However, the way fans enjoy *all-female heterosexual romances* needs to be unpacked. In this Element, I argue that women performing romances for ardent female fans creates a space for queer intimacy. The fact that the company and audiences appear to disregard the lesbian overtones of the performances helps to open a safe space to experience unconventional gender and sexual performance without being stigmatized as queer. This safe space is particularly important because gender and sexual conservativism still prevail in Japanese society at large.

As I explore how Takarazuka opens up the space for female same-sex intimacy, my approach is informed by and rooted in feminist and queer performance theory. Although the company mainly stages conventional romances, the productions selected for analysis in Sections 2 and 3 are more experimental and deviate from the heteronormative love story: *The Poe Clan* directed by Koike Shūichirō (Section 2) depicts a male homoerotic relationship that can be seen as a façade for female queer kinship; Section 3 explores works by the company's female director Ueda Kumiko (tenure from 2006 to 2022). The latter highlight Ueda's designs on protesting the capitalist management of

Takarazuka, thereby opening up an anti-capitalist space created through the queer bodies of performers, in and through which female same-sex intimacy is rendered a possibility. These case studies demonstrate the possibilities of female intimacy residing in different kinds of romance stories and a demand from the female audience for works that exhibit this theme. The remainder of this section sets the scene for the queer-orientated analysis of the shows, firstly by providing historical and contextualizing detail about the company and thereafter by outlining how queer intimacy is obscured and yet palpable in the company's adoption of two-dimensional performance aesthetics.

1.1 Fantasy, That Is Takarazuka

The first production of the Takarazuka Revue[3] took place in 1914, and it was one of many girls' companies that provided entertainment around the turn of the century.[4] It was founded in 1913 by an industrialist, Kobayashi Ichizō, to attract households along the Minō Arima Electric Railway (Minō Arima denki kidō, the precursor of Hankyu) to the spa near Takarazuka Station in a suburb of industrial Osaka. Kobayashi also pioneered the development of department stores at railroad stations; his company has become the Hankyu Hanshin Toho Group, which includes theatres, films, railways, department stores, hotels, and many more businesses. Hankyu's group enterprise publishes magazines about Takarazuka's performers and productions and runs a cable channel to broadcast its shows. A production usually consists of an hour-and-a-half-long musical and an hour-long revue. Many shows are original, but the company also adapts Western and Asian musicals as well as manga (graphic novels), computer games, and films from different parts of the world. Scriptwriters, directors, composers, orchestras, indeed all creatives needed for productions are resourced in-house. The company's headquarters are in Takarazuka City in Hyogo Prefecture, where it has the Takarazuka Grand Theater and the Bow Hall; in Tokyo the Takarazuka Theater is located in the centre of the capital.

The company is supported by its overwhelmingly female fan base. Fans often attend the same show multiple times, travel to various venues for its shows, and purchase photographs, DVDs, and other memorabilia. Performers specialize in either male or female roles, and male-role players (*otokoyaku*) are more popular than female-role players (*musumeyaku*). The most popular male-role players are

---

[3] It originally started as the Takarazuka Choir (Takarazuka shōkatai). After a few name changes, in 1940 it settled on the Takarazuka Revue.

[4] Many similar girls' companies were established following Takarazuka's success (Kurahashi & Tsuji 2005), but only Takarazuka and OSK Nippon Revue Company (formerly known as Osaka Shōchiku Kagekidan) are still in operation. While they were rivals in their earlier years, the latter is less well known and operates on a much smaller scale today.

those appointed by the management as the 'top stars'. Each of the five troupes – Flower (Hana), Moon (Tsuki), Snow (Yuki), Star (Hoshi), and Cosmos (Sora) – has its own top star who plays the protagonist in its shows.[5] Takarazuka thus employs the star system and protagonists are always male characters. A top star, or a top male-role player, forms a top *konbi* (from the English 'combination') with a top female-role player, and they perform a romantic couple in a heterosexual love story on stage. However, the top female-role player in each troupe is not accorded the same status as the top male-role player.

Performers receive two years of training at the Takarazuka Music School (Takarazuka ongaku gakkō, TMS) before starting their careers in the company. Their gender role is assigned upon entrance to the TMS based on their preference but also on their height; 5.4 feet is the minimum for male-role players (Takarazuka Music School n.d.: 3). Their gender roles are fixed during their tenure at the company, and marked by hairstyles, outfits, make-up, voice, and movements (see Figure 2).[6] Female-role players wear skirts and have long hair. They use pinkish foundation, eyeshadow, and blusher and have narrow, round eyebrows. They perform with high-pitched voices to depict either suave, elegant demeanours or more coquettish mannerisms. Male-role players wear trousers and have shorter hair. They have straight and thicker eyebrows and wear darker-coloured eye shadow and foundation.[7] They use low-pitched voices and learn to make larger, expansive movements.[8] This gender marking is strictly observed not just onstage but also in a performer's public life offstage (e.g., male-role players do not wear skirts in public).

The rigidity or fixity of gender-role assignment contrasts with the early years of Takarazuka when performers were able to play both female and male characters. It was in the 1930s when the company's repertoire shifted from folk tales to romances that the importance of those who could perform male characters increased and the strict gender-role division was implemented. It was around this time that the audience constituency also changed. Initially, the audience was a mix of men and women, but later women began to dominate

---

[5] In addition to these troupes, the company has a group of experienced performers who perform mainly old characters in the productions of all troupes. The group is called *senka*, the literal translation of which is 'specialized division', while it is officially translated as 'Superior Members'.

[6] There are some cases in which male-role players switch to female-role players but not the other way around. This seems to be based on the idea that women can naturally perform women while they require long-term training to perform men.

[7] But at the TMS, all the students, regardless of their gender roles, wear the school uniform with skirts, while male-role students wear short hair and female-role students put up their long hair in a chignon.

[8] Elizabeth York (2021) compares Takarazuka's performance style with that of Broadway musicals in her informative and insightful article.

Figure 2 Posters of productions at the Takarazuka Grand Theater. Right: *Golden Liberty* and *Phoenix Rising* (2024–2025) by the Moon Troupe. Left: *110 Years of Takarazuka Love Songs* (*Takarazuka 110 nen koi no uta*) and *Razzle Dazzle* (2025) by the Cosmos Troupe (photo taken by the author).

the audience due to their fascination with the male-role players (Kawasaki 1999: 161, 175, 188). All the performers, regardless of their gender roles, are called Takarasiennes (Takarajen'nu) after Parisiennes, reminiscent of the earlier influence of the French revue.

Japanese culture is hierarchical with students in schools typically using terms that denote their hierarchical relationship (e.g., *senpai* meaning senior, *kōhai* meaning junior). As in most schools, Takarasiennes learn to be obedient to those who are senior to them at the TMS. The strictness of the hierarchy can be seen in the documentary film about the company, *Dream Girls* (1994) by Kim Longinotto and Jano Williams, where junior students are shown bowing and loudly greeting senior students as each senior student enters the practice room. Although Takarasiennes are all women, as previously noted, male-role players are higher in the hierarchy than female-role players. For example, in an interview in *Dream Girls*, a female-role player talks about the need to obey male-role players, and a male-role player agrees with her, saying that patriarchy in the real world was recreated in the relationship between male- and female-role players. Patriarchalism is also ingrained in the Takarazuka institution: a gender hierarchy governs relations between the predominantly male management and the Takarasiennes. Takarazuka officially adopts the 'school' system where the management 'educates' Takarasiennes as their 'students'. When they start their training at the TMS between sixteen and nineteen years of age, they are naturally called students. However, they are still called students after they enter the company and up until they retire (typically in their late twenties to early thirties). In its education, the management instils in Takarasiennes a military-like notion of obedience; as shown in *Dream Girls*, they are taught how to do military-type marching by members of the Self-Defence Force as part of the group behaviour training. The documentary was released more than thirty years ago, but the environment it depicts largely remains the same today (see also Section 3).

Another way that Takarazuka operates as a school, rather than a place of work, is that Takarasiennes are required to retire from the company once they marry. The TMS, where Takarasiennes begin their 'studentship', was established by Kobayashi in 1919 following the success of the company, and although students received training in theatre arts, they were also 'schooled' as future wives and mothers of 'good Japanese citizens' in Japan's nation-building. As such, marriage and work in theatre were not seen as compatible, so married students had to retire to focus on their domestic labour as wives and mothers. Thus Takarazuka is not designed as a place where one can have a lifelong career, and even today, the rule of retirement upon marriage persists. Furthermore, with its famous motto of 'Modesty, Fairness, Grace' (*kiyoku tadashiku utsukushiku*), Takarazuka used to be seen as a finishing school for girls. This view is echoed in the Japanese term for female-role players, which is *musumeyaku*, meaning girl-role players. In this context, Takarasiennes were not considered 'professional' performers, and to this day, it promotes their amateurishness, even though many are skilled artists.[9] However, recent years have seen progress with Takarasiennes 'graduating' to pursue professional careers in show business or other fields of work.

In tandem with the management's conservative governance, 'setting' Takarazuka as a traditional girls' school in the small, idyllic city of Takarazuka also contributes to the company's business strategy of evoking nostalgia and maintaining the image of a fantasy world detached from reality in time and space.[10] This strategy is reflected in the shows, most of which are set in foreign countries in the past, as well as evinced in the image of Takarasiennes as 'fairies who sell dreams' (*yume o uru yōsei tachi*), the phrase first used in a number in the musical *Glory to Takarasiennes* (*Takarajen'nu ni eikō are*), written and directed by Takagi Shirō in 1962. A divorce from reality also occurs through the

---

[9] Takarasiennes' status as students also helped to distinguish them from *geisha*, professional female artists in traditional Japanese performance associated with pleasure quarters.

[10] As Kawasaki Kenko (2022: 201–214) argues, Takarazuka already commodified nostalgia in its formative years to reflect the public's longing for what they felt they had lost in the rapid social changes in the modern years. Lyrics of the songs were peppered with words such as 'missing' (*natsukashī*), 'remember dearly' (*omoi o haseru*), and 'faraway home' (*furusato*).

company's non-disclosure of Takarasiennes' ages and real names. Upon entering the company, Takarasiennes are known by their stage names, chosen in consultation with the TMS. These names are distinctively Takarazuka-esque to the ears and eyes of Japanese speakers. They often contain Chinese characters signifying the names of flowers as well as dance and sound (Takarazuka Music School n. d.: 5), though some Takarasiennes choose Western names such as Tomu (Tom) or Juria (Julia). Furthermore, information about their real life such as their salaries and romantic and sexual relationships is restricted by an informal set of guidelines enforced by the company and recognized by fans. These guidelines are called the violet code (*sumire kōdo*, named after Takarazuka's symbol flower). This code also restricts overly sexual scenes and other forms of 'vulgarity' in performances. All these serve to emphasize the fictionality of Takarazuka life, allowing the performance of same-sex heterosexual romance to appear as a harmless fantasy of a 'school drama club'.

Nonetheless, this notion of a fantasy world set in a girls' school entails a subversive possibility. As I have argued in my monograph (Anan 2016), girls' schools constituted a site where female students imagined, explored, and practised queer ways of being and loving, a phenomenon that persisted until the mid twentieth century when co-education became prevalent after World War II. Romantic relationships between schoolgirls, called *S* relationships (*esu kankei*, where *S* was short for 'sister'), were common. These relationships were serious and there were cases of double suicides committed by girls who were in despair at not being able to continue their relationships once they entered heteronormative society upon graduation. These love suicides made some think that *S* relationships threatened the social order, while others thought that these relationships were mere 'rehearsals' for heterosexual relationships that girls would experience in the future. Schoolgirls took advantage of this latter view of 'mere rehearsals' as a façade: they did not publicly protest it, but rather beneath this façade developed what I call resistant 'girls' aesthetics'. They not only practised *S* relationships but also explored resistance in their fantasy. This fantasy appeared similar to that constructed by the conservative Takarazuka management, but schoolgirls twisted it for their own purpose. The 'stage' for their fantasy was girls' magazines. In readers' columns and short stories, schoolgirls created images of themselves as eternal girls existing outside of teleological time to resist the developmental paradigm, or adult womanhood-cum-heteronormativity, that shaped their lives. They also performed fictional selves by using beautiful pen names as if to leave their material reality as future wives and mothers behind. They even fantasized about death as the ultimate way to remain girls. Girls' double suicides may be considered as a realization of this fantasy.

Importantly, articles about Takarasiennes and their photographs were popular content in these magazines. I do not have space here to trace a history of girls' aesthetics to the present, but what is important in this introductory section and overall in this Element is that female audience members can imagine prolonging their queer and resistant girlhood through Takarazuka. Fans can imagine themselves being part of this girls' school by frequenting the theatres and familiarizing themselves with its 'students' through its publicity materials. Fans, and perhaps Takarasiennes as well, can take advantage of the 'harmless' fantasy world of Takarazuka to explore female queer intimacy without being identified as queer. Takarazuka thus fulfils a 'double duty' as a musical company, as identified by Stacy Wolf (2002: viii) in her discussion of female stars as gay icons in mid twentieth-century Broadway musicals; musicals, as part of the mainstream culture, convey conservative values, but '[d]esiring spectators ... can readily interpret musicals in ways that stress women's power and de-emphasize heterosexual romance'. Like these Broadway musicals, Takarazuka productions 'contain both explicit and covert allusions to queerness' (viii–ix).

It is important to mention here that I consider queerness in terms of intensity and unlocatability of non-normative affects and desires. My view is informed by Xavier Aldana Reyes (2018: 125), who suggests that queer is 'a political label that expresses difference in sexual desire, a more open and non-specific non-heteronormative form of desire and identity'. Thus I do not consider only homosexuality as queer based on the static binary of either homosexual or heterosexual. I also do not limit the sexual and erotic to the involvement of genital pleasure. Some researchers of Japanese girls' culture, who draw a clear line between girls' homosexuality and their intimate friendship, base their arguments on the involvement of genital pleasure or the lack thereof (Shamoon 2012; Yamanashi 2012). Contrastingly, I argue that bodily sensations and affects are incited and experienced through various forms of caring interactions (such as exchanging love letters, typically practised by those in *S* relationships) and that they may not always be qualitatively different from those made available by genital love. Takarazuka, as a girls' school, is where fans can fantasize such a range of intimacy.

1.2 Two-Dimensional Bodies of Takarasiennes

In addition to these introductory details about Takarazuka, the Element's focus on the idea of all-female intimacy also requires some further, brief contextualization regarding recent debates about the company.[11] These concern the dimensionality and layering of Takarasiennes' bodies.

---

[11] For international readers less familiar with Takarazuka the following book-length studies in English are useful: anthropologist Jennifer Robertson's *Takarazuka: Sexual Politics and Popular*

Takarazuka frequently adapts manga, and this invites comparison with the 2.5-dimensional theatre (*2.5 jigen butai*), which is a stage adaptation of two-dimensional media such as manga, anime, and games that has become increasingly popular since the early 2000s in Japan and beyond. Realistic acting can be seen as a tool for the three-dimensionalization of characters in that it gives them *depth*. By contrast, in two-dimensional media, characters are flat and lack real-world depth. In adapting these two-dimensional media for the stage, performance that attempts to be too realistic can lose its connection to the source material. Thus the goal of 2.5-dimensional theatre is to bridge the actors' three-dimensional bodies and the two-dimensional sources, and this in-between state creates what media scholar Sugawa Akiko (2021: 18–19) calls 'virtual corporeality'. Musicals are a mainstay of this genre, even though characters do not sing and dance in the source material, and this consequently inspires comparison with Takarazuka. The company is indeed a pioneer of stage adaptations of manga, dating back to *Shō-chan's Adventure* (*Shō-chan no bōken*) in 1924.[12] Sugawa (2021: 51) also observes that the company's 1974 production of *The Rose of Versailles* (*Berusaiyu no bara*) anticipated the arrival of 2.5-dimensional theatre with its reproduction of the visual aspects of the characters in the original manga.[13] A similarity between the two genres is further suggested by the way in which some Takarasiennes, after retiring from the company, perform in 2.5-dimensional theatre and that a former Takarazuka director, Kodama Akiko (tenure from 1997 to 2013), now works in this genre. Nonetheless, there are some differences. For example, 2.5-dimensional theatre tries to create exact reproductions of the original images, including even minute details such as the waves of a character's hair (Azuma 2016: 84). Contrastingly, although Takarazuka seeks to imitate the original manga's images to a certain extent, its primary aim is to highlight the virtuosity and

---

Culture in Modern Japan (1998); sociologist Leonie R. Stickland's *Gender Gymnastics: Performing and Consuming Japan's Takarazuka Revue* (2008); and theatre scholar Makiko Yamanashi's *A History of Takarazuka Revue since 1914: Modernity, Girls' Culture, Japan Pop* (2012). Yamanashi also recently published *Performing Cross-Cultural Modernity: Behind and beyond Japan's Takarazuka Revue* (2023). There are many Japanese-language academic books on the company, including several by literature and theatre scholar Kawasaki Kenko. All these are highly informative, with detailed discussions about the company's development, often with a focus on particular periods and/or a particular genre (such as revue). Among them, Yamanashi's perspective is heteronormative, but many others examine Takarazuka's potential for unconventional 'gender gymnastics'. However, confined to their respective disciplinary fields, these gender explorations are not grounded in performance theory, unlike my analysis in this Element.

[12] It is by Tōfūjin (aka Kabashima Katsuichi) and Oda Shōsei and printed in *Asahi Graph* and *Asahi Shimbun* with slight modifications of the title from 1923 to 1926.

[13] It is by Ikeda Riyoko and serialized in *Margaret* from 1972 to 1973. The theatre adaptation is Takarazuka's signature show and I will touch on it in Section 2.

attraction of its top stars. Fans attend the shows not to see the characters but to see the top stars and other Takarasiennes.

This begins to explain why I argue that the notion of 2.5 dimensions does not apply to Takarazuka's performance. My view is closer to that of Koyanagi Naoko (EUREKA Editorial Department 2015), a Takarazuka director who often creates manga-based shows. In an interview, she says that the company's performance is '2.4-dimensional'. She does not clearly explain what the 0.1 difference suggests, but she may mean that Takarazuka deducts more from the three-dimensional bodies of performers than 2.5-dimensional theatre,[14] as she states, 'We are often asked why our male-role players are so cool. The reason is that they don't add coolness [to their bodies] but take out uncoolness [from them]. Instead of releasing a nice scent, they try to remove any smell' (133). She mentions male-role players as an example, arguably because their fictionality is more visible than female-role players', but considering that Takarazuka is a fantasy world, all Takarasiennes' bodies may be less than 2.5-dimensional. I would go further and propose, as I did in my earlier work (Anan 2011; Anan 2016), that Takarasiennes' bodies are two-dimensional. Fictionality or fantasy is supported by the immateriality of Takarasiennes' bodies.

Whether it is 2.4 or 2.5, the decimals are predicated on the assumption, particularly of media and manga scholars writing about 2.5-dimensional theatre, that bodies on stage are normally three-dimensional. However, the bodily presence of actors is not always seen as such in theatre and performance studies. For example, inspired by visual artist Murakami Takashi's theorization of Japanese arts, culture, and society being 'super-flat', theatre/performance scholar Tadashi Uchino (2009: 128) has conceptualized the super-flat 'junk body' of practitioners in Japanese experimental performance in the late 1990s and early 2000s. While the previous generations used either language (modern realist theatre) or body (the 1960s experimental theatre) as an artistic and political tool to challenge the status quo both of society and of theatre arts, young practitioners were deprived of these tools under neoliberal sovereignty where the identity of those who exploited them was obscured; they only had their junk bodies that were 'physically present, burdened with nothing'. Such bodies 'betray[ed] and exhibit[ed] the postmodern rupture between language and the body by using super-flat surfaces on which diverse simulacra are projected' (133).

---

[14] As Iwashita Hōsei points out, 0.5 of 2.5 dimensions is tricky; 2.5 may be a result of the deduction of some quality from three-dimensional human bodies or the addition of some quality to two-dimensional characters. For detailed discussion, see his monograph, *When Characters Become Real* (*Kyara ga riaru ni naru toki*) (Iwashita 2020).

Comparably, I also see Takarasiennes' bodies as 'physically present, burdened with nothing', but in their case, 'nothing' about essentialized gender and sexuality associated with their biologically female bodies. Takarasiennes' fictional bodies may be burdened with the conventional management's gender and sexual ethos, but these bodies also slip into two-dimensional surfaces on to which audiences can project various forms of queer desires and sentiments. This is also enhanced by their over-the-top, excessive performance style, which rejects the realist mode of meaning-making. In this regard, Takarasiennes' bodies exemplify feminist mimesis as theorized by Elin Diamond, a theorization inspired by Luce Irigaray's deconstructive reading of Plato's myth of the cave. In the *Republic*, he conceived reflections on the wall of the cave as 'a metaphor for the illusory nature of worldly objects that keep man from contemplating true Forms, the unseeable Ideal' (Diamond 1997: xi). Irigaray points out Plato's association of deceptiveness, or mimesis, with a woman whose womb/cave is impregnated with it and reconfigures this cave as a 'womb-theater' – that is, 'illusionistic apparatus' that 'obscure[s] the mode of production'; those in this 'theater' cannot see the origins of the reflections and therefore take reflections as the origins – hence, 'mimesis without truth' (Diamond 1997: xi). Even when this womb/cave opens for men to see the Truth/Ideal outside, what is delivered with them is 'fake offspring' (xii), and therefore, what is in the world outside the cave is also 'mimesis without truth'. Takarasiennes, who are 'physically present, burdened with nothing' are 'fake offspring'.

Arguing for the flatness of Takarasiennes' bodies is also supported by sociologist Azuma Sonoko's notion of the 'Takarasienne's four-layered structure'. She was inspired by Kawasaki Kenko, a pioneer of Takarazuka studies, who describes how 'a Takarasienne performs her role in plays, a gender-role of either male or female, a Takarasienne, and herself as a student' (Kawasaki 1999: 196). Azuma (2015: 96) proposes that a Takarasienne consists of the four layers of her 'existence': 'role-name existence', 'stage-name existence', 'nickname existence', and 'real-name existence'. The first two involve her performance onstage, and the latter two offstage. Within the story of a show, she exists as a role or a character, hence, 'role-name existence'. 'Stage-name existence' implies her qualities and characteristics as a Takarasienne, including her status and gender role within the company. Offstage, Takarasiennes call each other by their nicknames. Fans familiarize themselves with these nicknames from the company's publicity materials and also use them to refer to Takarasiennes as though fans were their classmates. Fans enjoy this 'nickname existence' as a Takarasienne's 'natural' existence, despite being fully aware that this is part of the public performance. 'Real-name existence' is what fans cannot access; Takarasiennes' real names are not disclosed, as previously noted, but also, who she is other than being a Takarasienne is unknown (83–96).[15]

These layers of existence, except the 'real-name existence', are mobilized in a show. As an example, Azuma cites the Flower Troupe's revue show *Cocktail* (written and directed by Fujii Daisuke in 2002). The top star Takumi Hibiki performed the role of a star artist named Charlie ('role-name existence') in some scenes, where he dances with his colleagues at a bar named Charlie's. This is his last appearance at the bar and he fondly recalls his former days. On the metatheatrical level, *Cocktail* was Takumi's last production for Takarazuka ('stage-name existence'), and her nickname was Charlie ('nickname existence') (Azuma 2015: 83–84). Thus, to fully understand Takarazuka's shows, familiarity with these layers is required. Azuma's usage of the term 'layer' (*sō*) might suggest that we initially access a Takarasienne's performance via the 'role-name existence' and that we *deepen* our understanding of her performance as we familiarize ourselves with other layers of her existence. However, as this example demonstrates, these layers unfold together, merging into one surface for fans to make sense of the show. Moreover, even if we could go deep *down*, what awaits us is the layer of their 'real-name existence', which is unknown to us. Takarasiennes as signifiers do not have a signified – or at least, they do not rest on a single signified. In short, they are two-dimensional, an understanding that informs my analysis in the following sections as I explore how immaterial Takarasiennes perform as a medium through which female audience members might fantasize and experience various forms of all-female intimacy.

2 Female Queer Kinship and *The Poe Clan*

Although Takarazuka's romances are typically heterosexual, queer characters do appear. They represent three patterns: intense friendship, homoeroticism, and homosexuality. The most common pattern is an intense friendship between a male protagonist and another male character as part of a musical's story. In revues which have no coherent storylines or characters, homoerotic scenes frequently appear when male-role players perform sensual interactions as a duo. These suggest that the company sees male intimacy as an important demand of the female audience. However, the musicals and revues tend to exclude homosexual *relationships*. If a homosexual relationship were to be

---

[15] Leonie R. Stickland (2008: 112–113) makes a similar point. She identifies three 'faces' of a Takarasienne: a 'gendered "face" … of the character a Takarasienne enacts within the confines of the proscenium arch', her '"public" face, which she shows to fans and the Takarazuka-savvy general populace when she identifies herself as a Takarasienne', and a '"private" face for herself, her intimate friends and family, or, on the other hand, for total strangers who are not aware of her occupation'.

placed at the centre of a story, it would 'risk' highlighting female bodies performing male homosexuality and, in turn, female homosexual relationships that potentially underlie Takarasiennes' performance of male characters.[16] In brief, it is difficult to present homosexual relationships on the Takarazuka stage.

The Poe Clan (*Pō no ichizoku*) (2018), written and directed by Koike Shūichirō and performed by the Flower Troupe, is a story about an intense friendship between two vampire boys, and it highlights male homoeroticism. The show is atypical in that it is an adaptation of the famous manga that depicts all three patterns of queer intimacy including homosexual elements. This section discusses this work as a reflection on and exemplification of how a queer relationship between two vampire boys can be seen as mirroring female queer intimacy in Takarazuka.

2.1 *The Poe Clan* and *Shōnen-ai* Manga

The Poe Clan by Hagio Moto was printed in a girls' manga magazine, *Bessatsu Shōjo Comic*, between 1972 and 1976. Set in various places in Europe from the eighteenth to the twentieth centuries, the story centres on a vampire boy, Edgar, who travels with another boy, Alan, whom he turned into a vampire.[17] They do not label themselves as lovers, but there is an erotic charge to their relationship.[18] For example, unlike most vampires who consume the blood of their victims, Alan prefers to suck blood from Edgar. This is presented sensuously in the manga: Alan is depicted embracing Edgar, his lips approaching Edgar's neck. This transfer of blood is akin to the transfer of fluid during sex. Also, as Hagio notes, Alan's demand for Edgar's exclusive attention demonstrates his romantic attachment to Edgar.[19] In the last episode in the manga, Alan accidentally perishes in a fire; a devastated Edgar also disappears into the fire.[20]

---

[16] The company has very few productions that feature female intimacy. *Nova Bossa Nova*, a revue show written and directed by Kamogawa Seisaku and produced multiple times since 1971, has a sensuous scene at a female-only club. In the company's adaptation of a Broadway musical, *Grand Hotel* (directed by Tommy Tune and Okada Keiji in 1993 and Okada and Ikuta Hirokazu in 2017), Raffaela loves Elizaveta as in the original. *The Rose of Versailles*, written and directed by Ueda Shinji and produced many times since 1974, has a woman character in love with another woman as in the original girls' manga.

[17] The characters' names are obviously from Edgar Allan Poe, but this simply seems a play on words. There is no direct connection between this manga and Poe's work, although they do share Gothic and romantic elements.

[18] Some find that the relationship between Edgar and Alan is similar to the relationship between Lestat and Louis in Ann Rice's *Interview with the Vampires* (1976) (Kakinuma 2007: 60; Miyabe 1998: 299; Satō 2007: 20, 24). However, it is not clear if Hagio and Rice knew each other's work.

[19] *BL shinkaron saron tōku tokubetsuhen* [Special Talk: Salon for Theorizing BL as a Transformative Genre] (2020) https://note.com/howdy90/n/n3bffc3ad0765 (accessed 13 May 2024).

[20] This left readers wondering if he committed suicide. (Although vampires have eternal life, they can perish in a fire.) However, in 2016, Hagio surprised her manga readership by starting a sequel

The Poe Clan is a representative work of 'boys' love' manga, a subgenre of girls' manga targeting young female readers. Before the late 1960s, girls' manga predominantly consisted of heteronormative romances and comedies for female adolescents produced by male artists. However, in the 1970s, a group of female manga artists called the Year 24 Group (Nijūyo nen gumi, so named because they were born around the twenty-fourth year of the reign of the Shōwa Emperor, or AD 1949) created 'boys' love' (*shōnen-ai*) manga, which introduced concerns about body, gender, and sexuality into the genre and expanded its readership beyond female teens. This genre was the precursor of what after the 1990s is called the 'Boys' Love' or BL genre, pronounced in Japanized English as *bōizu rabu* or *bīéru*. The BL genre has evolved into a predominantly light-hearted manga involving adult couples and many works are sexually explicit. By contrast, the original boys' love genre, which I will refer to as *shōnen-ai* to avoid confusion with BL, portrayed relationships between boys in a serious literary tone influenced by figures such as Hermann Hesse, Jean Genet, and Inagaki Taruho.

Although *shōnen-ai* manga depicted boys' relationships, boys were portrayed as androgynous or even girlie. As I argued elsewhere (Anan, 2016), these androgynous boys can be considered as girls in disguise or as alter egos. Also, considering that *shōnen-ai* manga was often set in the idealized West, the genre functioned as a medium for female artists and readers to experiment with an identity as Western boys on the narrative level, while retaining female bodies unaffected by conventional gender roles such as wife and mother in Japan (i.e., a reproducer of 'good' Japanese citizens). In other words, material reality is imaginatively removed from their bodies. Thus, boys in *shōnen-ai* manga are immaterial girls who experience same-sex intimacy. Importantly, the immaterial nature of these girls resonates with the 'two-dimensional' bodies of Takarasiennes, as discussed in Section 1. Moreover, girls in the guise of boys equate with male-role players. Like androgynous boys in *shōnen-ai* manga, male-role players do not try to look realistically like men; they perform masculine mannerisms but do not aim to pass as men. These are suggestive of what underlies Takarazuka fans' fascination with male same-sex intimacy: what they witness through the intimacy performed by male-role players is female same-sex intimacy.

2.2 *The Poe Clan* and Koike Shūichirō

Koike Shūichirō, who adapted *The Poe Clan* for the Takarazuka stage, has been a fan of this manga ever since he read it on the recommendation of his women friends at university. Since 1977 when he embarked on his career at Takarazuka, he

---

in which Edgar, who seemingly survived the fire, embarks on a journey to find a way to resurrect Alan. The sequel was ongoing as of December 2024.

has repeatedly expressed a wish to stage it with the company (Koike 1998: 298; Koike 2018a: 5). He praises its aesthetic quality and theme, such as the inquiry into the meaning of life and death (Koike 1998: 299; Koike 2018a: 5), but he desexualizes the relationship between Edgar and Alan. In an interview released in 2021, Koike said that he was aware that this manga was in the category of BL (meaning *shōnen-ai*), but what moved him was the two lone, 'vulnerable' 'souls' which 'resonate with each other' and 'unite their destinies' (Koike 2021). Explaining why he had to wait forty years to stage the adaptation, Koike stated that it was because he had been unable to find male-role players who could perform the eternal fourteen-year-old vampires (2018a: 5). On the one hand, performances by Asumi Rio and Yuzuka Rei were worth the wait (see Figure 3); in particular, Asumi, celebrated as 'the top of tops' with her 'fairy-like grace' and excellence in acting and singing, received many positive reviews for her performance of Edgar (Katō 2019: 17; Miyamoto 2019: 4, 24; Yabushita 2019: 9). On the other hand, it is arguably the case that the original manga's status as an iconic *shōnen-ai* manga also accounts for the delayed acquiescence on the part of the company's management. Even when the adaptation was finally produced, it was promoted on the company's website as a stage adaptation of a monumental manga by a respected artist, Hagio Moto, in which a sad but beautiful and mysterious story of vampire youth unfolds – no mention of its queerness.[21]

A few other atypical productions helped pave the way for *The Poe Clan*. A case in point is *Nijinsky* (2011), a musical written and directed by Harada Ryō and performed by the Snow Troupe. The central drive of its story was the love-and-hate relationship between Vaslav Nijinsky (played by Sagiri Seina) and Sergei Diaghilev (Ozuki Tōma). The portrayal of this relationship involved kissing (though note that Takarasiennes only ever simulate kissing) and verbalization of their regular engagement in sex.[22] This work retains a heterosexual element as it also portrays Nijinsky's relationship with his wife, Romola (Manaka Ayu), and as Tamaki Yasuko (2011: 72) points out, the 'genuine love' of this marriage is contrasted with the love-and-hate relationship between

---

[21] *Takarazuka Revue* (2018). https://kageki.hankyu.co.jp/revue/2018/ponoichizoku/info.html (accessed 18 December 2024). Many of Hagio's works have been adapted for the stage, and the first adaptation of her work at Takarazuka was *American Pie* (2003) by Koyanagi Naoko. The original manga was released in 1976, and it is Hagio's non-*shōnen-ai* manga about male-female friendship. Centring on friendship rather than romance is unusual in Takarazuka.

[22] The first time that male homosexual acts by minor characters featured on the Takarazuka stage was in *Revolt of Prince Hayabusawake* (*Hayabusawake ōji no hanran*) (1978), adapted from Tanabe Seiko's novel and directed by Ako Ken and performed by the Moon Troupe; a male character in love with the heterosexual protagonist (fake) kissed him on his lips while he was sleeping (Kotake 2005: 196). As Kotake Satoshi (197) observes, this virtually coincides with the emergence of *shōnen-ai* manga.

Figure 3 Flyer of *The Poe Clan* (Right: Asumi Rio as Edgar. Left: Yuzuka Rei as Alan. Lower left: Senna Ayase as Sheila) (photo taken by the author).

Nijinsky and Diaghilev. Nonetheless, this production is distinctive for its depiction of a protagonist involved in a homosexual relationship.

Another factor relating to the management's decision to finally stage *The Poe Clan* was, as Iwamoto Taku (2020: 57) notes, Koike's status as one of the leading musical directors in Takarazuka and beyond.[23] An award-winning director, Koike's most significant contribution to the Japanese musical scene is his introduction and adaptation of large-scale Western musicals such as *Elisabeth, Mozart!, The Scarlet Pimpernel*, and *1789 Les Amants de la Bastille*.[24] He also successfully adapted manga and film for theatre. *The Poe Clan* was staged as a so-called *ippon mono*. In Takarazuka jargon, this means that the production consists only of a musical; there is no accompanying revue show. This arrangement is reserved for what the company considers to be its major representative shows, many of which are by Koike. Note that, unlike *Nijinsky*, which was staged at the Bow Hall, a smaller venue for experimental works and works by emerging directors, *The Poe Clan* was presented in the Takarazuka Grand Theater, the company's main theatre.

2.3 Queer Kinship of the Takarazuka Clan: Blood, Bond, and Poe

Staged in the Grand Theater, Takarazuka's *The Poe Clan* is based on two episodes from the original manga that depict boys who lost their places in their respective families and the process by which they turn into vampires. Edgar and his younger sister, Marybelle (played by Hana Yūki), are born to a British earl and his mistress, but the earl's jealous wife devises a stratagem to kill them. They are left alone in the forests to die, but are found and raised by the vampire clan of Poe in a village named Scotty. When Edgar is fourteen, the clan's mansion is assaulted by villagers. To sustain the blood of the clan, the patriarch, King Poe (Itsuki Chihiro), turns Edgar into a vampire and Edgar later turns Marybelle into one too. Forced out of the village, the siblings travel from one place to another with clan members and a married couple, Frank (Seto Kazuya) and Sheila (Senna Ayase), as their 'parents'.[25] In 1879, the vampire family arrives in Blackpool, where Edgar meets Alan and develops a friendship with him. However, everyone

---

[23] In Takarazuka, directors normally write the scripts for shows they direct, but they are only referred to as directors, a convention I observe in this Element.

[24] *Elisabeth* (first produced for Takarazuka in 1996) is the most well known of his works; he received multiple awards for this production. For his adaptation of this Viennese musical, he changed the protagonist from Elisabeth to Death in accordance with the Takarazuka convention that dictates that the main male character is performed by a top male-role player. This version is frequently revived by the company. Koike also often directs this musical outside Takarazuka with Elisabeth as the protagonist performed by former female-role players.

[25] Senna was the top female-role player who normally played a romantic partner of a male protagonist played by Asumi Rio. In this production, Edgar's 'romantic' partner is Alan, and he is performed by Yuzuka Rei, the second-positioned male-role player. To keep an element of a 'couple' between Asumi and Senna, Edgar's crush on Sheila is very briefly depicted in this production, while there is no such episode in the original manga. As in the original manga, Alan has a crush on Marybell. However, regardless of their crush on these female characters, they are bonded with each other in a queer manner.

but Edgar in the family perishes in the chaos caused by humans who have discovered they are vampires. Unable to bear the loneliness, Edgar invites Alan to join him in a goalless journey. Alan, who has been isolated in his dysfunctional family, where his uncle tries to control him and take over the business of his dead father, agrees and allows Edgar to turn him into a vampire. The story ends with a brief scene where the boys, as transfer students, attend a secondary school in Cologne, Germany in 1959, suggesting that they have been travelling together across time and space with their destinies united.

Prominent in the Takarazuka version is its emphasis on notions of clan and bloodline. 'You will join the Poe clan' (Koike 2018b: 65), says Edgar to Alan when he turns him into a vampire, a clan that King Poe declares needs to 'increase family members. We need new blood' (60). Also, Sheila and Frank respectively tell Edgar that he 'inherits King Poe's blood as the future leader of the clan' (52) and that they are 'bonded by the blood of the clan' (51). On the one hand, valuing clan, family, and bloodline is conservative and reactionary, and King Poe's command to 'increase family members' is reminiscent of remarks by politicians worried about what they perceive as the decline of the 'Japanese race'.[26] However, significantly and crucially, the clan's blood relations are not based on heterosexual reproduction.

In her theorization of the lesbian vampire in relation to lesbian invisibility, Sue-Ellen Case (1991: 4) critiques heterosexuals' claim to blood as 'the right to life': 'The right to life was [historically] formulated through a legal, literary, and scientific discourse on blood, which stabilized privilege by affirming the right to life for those who could claim blood ... and the consequent death sentence, either metaphorically or literally, for those who could not'. Sustenance of the bloodline through heterosexual reproduction legitimates heterosexuals' 'right to life', but the vampires in *The Poe Clan* disrupt this sense of reproduction. They sustain their bloodline, but not through procreation. They share blood, but they are not related by birth. Vampiric blood relations embrace what conventional human kinship does not. In the original manga and stage versions, Edgar responds to the question about why vampires exist by saying, 'Why? If only I knew! Nothing to create. Nothing to give birth to. No legacy for generations to come' (Hagio 1998: 110; Koike 2018b: 64). In the Takarazuka staging, the answer lies in the centrality of the clan to the show's storyline: the emphasis on

---

[26] For example, many members of the Liberal Democratic Party (Jimintō, conservative despite its party name), which has been in power for most of the post-war years, are against gender equality and LGBTQ rights, as they see them as threats to the traditional family values that they believe sustain the 'Japanese race'.

familial bonds that are created and passed on outside of the traditional family and normative sexuality – that is, a kind of queer kinship.[27]

The show's storyline distinguishes between vampires and humans, but in performance the boundary between the two often blurs; eventually, they all appear as though encompassed in the 'clan'. One example of this differentiation to blurring of the human and vampiric occurs in a chorus number in Act 1, titled 'The Poe Clan', written jointly by Hagio and Koike and composed by Ōta Takeshi.[28] It starts with phrases sung by Edgar and other vampires that praise their Gothic beauty, such as 'Exquisite beauty, eternal life' and 'Deep in the misty forest/ Living in a garden full of roses', and towards the end, they are joined by human characters who sing lyrics slightly different from theirs: the vampires sing, 'We are the clan/ We stop time and live eternally' and the humans sing, 'They are the clan/ They stop time and live eternally'. The clan members and the others are differentiated here not only by lyrics but also by costumes; vampires are attired in eighteenth-century, English-styled costumes, while humans wear more contemporary suits and dresses. However, in terms of lyrics, it is difficult to hear the differences. In Japanese, 'we' (*warera*) and 'they' (*karera*) sound similar. As the number concludes with the phrase 'the Poe clan' (Koike 2018b: 47), sung by all with the same choreography, it sounds and appears as though they all belong to a single clan. Another example is the final scene at the German school, where human students are singing a popular song from the Billboard charts at the time, titled 'Lonely Vampires' (*Kanashimi no banpanera*), with the phrases 'I am a vampire/ I am a vampire' (66) as Edgar and Alan watch them. Thus the show starts and ends with a staging that allows a conception of the clan that includes all the characters, the vampires and the humans. To recall Azuma's theorization of layers of a Takarasienne's existence (see Section 1) is to see how this onstage clan is resonant with the clan-like community of Takarasiennes offstage. This is further emphasized by the similarity between the vampires, who are eternally beautiful and live outside of human society, and Takarasiennes, who continually recreate beautiful creatures onstage while living in the fantasy world of Takarazuka.

The queerness of the clan is first suggested by Edgar and Alan's dance to the chorus of 'The Poe Clan'. This chorus explains the history of the vampires as chronicled by human researchers whose ancestors met Edgar and Alan, a history recorded from the vantage point of 1964. As the researchers highlight key

---

[27] The founder of Takarazuka, Kobayashi Ichizō, conceived the Takarazuka institution as a family where he was the 'father' of Takarasiennes (Robertson 1998: 16). Like the Poe clan, this 'kinship' is not based on genetic relations, but it is an extension of a heteronormative family rather than an alternative kinship as seen in and through *The Poe Clan*.

[28] All the music numbers discussed in this section were composed by Ōta to Koike's lyrics, except for this one with lyrics jointly written by Hagio and Koike.

incidents from their records, these are mimed/danced by characters at the centre of the stage in front of others singing and dancing in the chorus. A dance sequence between the two boys accompanies the archivists' announcement, 'In 1879 . . . to the twilight and darkness, [Edgar] takes Alan' (Koike 2018b: 46–47) (meaning that Edgar turns Alan into a vampire). This includes sensual choreography: Edgar caresses Alan's chest from behind, Alan caresses Edgar's arm, and they touch each other's cheeks lovingly. This queerness is then expanded to other characters in a later chorus number, 'Two Souls: A World without Love' (*Futatsu no tamashī: ai no nai sekai*), which concludes Act 1. Initially, it appears to be about the loneliness experienced by Edgar and Alan, but as it progresses, the number encompasses other characters' search for love, as well as their celebration of love (despite the title). In the last scene of this act, Edgar and Alan learn about each other's loneliness and sympathize with each other. Edgar impulsively tries to reproduce Alan as a vampire to cure his loneliness but restrains himself. Then he sings about his longing for love: 'We cannot live without love/ Longing, wanting, wandering/ For days I love and am loved by someone'. As the number crescendos, he is joined by all the other characters, both vampires and humans. They take turns and sing; for example, Edgar singing 'Wishing to talk' is followed by Sheila singing 'With him, about our life together' (57), with her eyes lovingly on Frank. On the narrative level, both Edgar's intense feelings for Alan and Sheila's heterosexual love for Frank are presented in the sequence. However, intense male friendship and heterosexual romance do not appear to be clearly distinguished as the sequence is jointly sung by Edgar and Sheila, queerly nullifying a neat categorization of intimacy. Further supporting this reading is that it is women's bodies that sing and perform the sequence about love, whether it is intense friendship or romance, evoking a range of female intimacy.

In my conceptualization of this queer clan or kinship, fans play an important part. In the show, when Frank tells Edgar that they are 'bonded by the blood of the clan' (51), he uses the word *kizuna* (bond). Fans will know that Takarasiennes often use this word to describe the bond between a top male-role player and a top female-role player, as well as the bond among those who enter the TMS in the same year, same troupe or the whole company. Azuma (2015: 124–146) has maintained that a Takarasienne's layered existence allows fans to fantasize about the homosocial bond offstage through the heterosexual romance onstage. While she excludes other forms of queer intimacy, I argue that fans can fantasize about a range of intimacy or bonds.[29] This is also the case when the onstage performance is not a heterosexual romance, as evinced in *The Poe Clan*.

---

[29] To be fair to Azuma (2015: 123), she acknowledges that fans may fantasize a homosexual bond among Takarasiennes. However, she still insists that they largely comply with the violet code and interpret Takarasiennes' intimacy as only homosocial.

Female intimacy seen in Takarazuka's performance exemplifies the lesbian continuum conceptualized by Adrienne Rich. In her seminal essay, 'Compulsory Heterosexuality and Lesbian Existence', she explains:

> I mean the term *lesbian continuum* to include a range – through each woman's life and throughout history – of woman-identified experience; not simply the fact that a woman has had or consciously desired genital sexual experience with another woman. If we expand it to embrace many more forms of primary intensity between and among women, including the sharing of a rich inner life, the bonding against male tyranny, the giving and receiving of practical and political support ... we begin to grasp breadths of female history and psychology. (Rich 1980: 648–649; emphasis in original)

This conceptualization of the lesbian continuum was much contested because it was seen to be desexualizing and depoliticizing lesbians, or 'women who have made their primary and erotic and emotional choices for women' (Rich 1986: 73–74). Later, Rich herself showed an understanding of this critique; she endorsed it, acknowledging that the lesbian continuum could be appropriated by heterosexual feminists 'who have not yet begun to examine the privileges and solipsisms of heterosexuality, as a safe way to describe their felt connections with women, without having to share in the risks and threats of lesbian existence' (73). Ultimately, she dismissed 'Compulsory Heterosexuality and Lesbian Existence': 'I felt it flawed, outdated, and ... no longer representative of my thinking and the thinking I respected' (Rich 2004: 9). While I agree that the lesbian continuum entails risks, I still find it explains the range of female intimacy in Takarazuka. Fans witness the intimacy among female performers moving back and forth between lovers on stage and soulmates offstage, and this mesmerizing process of moving, moving with intensity, ignites affects and desires among fans that are not necessarily locatable within a single and fixed category. Such a range of affects and desires is difficult to experience outside Takarazuka given the dominant, heteronormative fabric of Japanese society.

2.4 Performing Kin

Over generations, Takarazuka has served as a space where non-normative intimacy has been performed by women, as though they belong to the 'Takarazuka clan'. In exploring this non-genetical, queer clanship, Elizabeth Freeman's theorization of queer kinship offers valuable insights, even though she equates queer only with homosexuality. She provides a way to consider kinship through *performance*. She writes about queer longing for kinship against the dominant idea that queer kinship is inconceivable because queer people lack a means of renewal – that is, procreation that enables a temporal extension (Freeman 2007: 297):

> To want to belong ... is to long to be bigger not only spatially, but also temporally, to 'hold out' a hand across time and touch the dead or those not born yet, to offer oneself beyond one's own time. Longing to belong, being long: these things encompass not only the desire to impossibly extend our individual existence or to preserve relationships that will invariably end, but also to have something queer exceed its own time, even to imagine that excess *as* queer in ways that getting married or having children might not be. (Freeman 2007: 299; emphasis in original)

In her theorization, Freeman is informed by the 'practical kinship' proposed by Pierre Bourdieu, which is 'the non-genealogical relationships which can be mobilized for the ordinary needs of existence' (Bourdieu cited in Freeman 2007: 308). Here, kinship is conceived as a 'set of *acts*' that is not necessarily predicated on the sharing of genetic substances (Freeman 2007: 305; emphasis in original). This model of kinship inspires Freeman in that it involves habitus, which enables 'non-reproductive corporeal transfer' (306). As 'learned bodily disposition, stance, or schema' (305), habitus 'communicates ... from body to body' (Bourdieu cited in Freeman 2007: 305), thereby bodies mimetically become similar and accustomed to each other. Moreover, this corporeal schema takes place not only in a space between and within bodies but also across time as habitus entails repetition or duration to be ingrained within a body (Freeman 2007: 305–306). Through habitus, therefore, bodily relations 'become long', or belongings generate and renew but not through genetical reproduction. As an example of queer mimetic bodies, Freeman cites the frequent gesture performed by lesbians captured in photographs in an exhibition of a homosexual history, 'Becoming Visible', held at the New York Public Library in 1994. The images of a lesbian 'lighting another's cigarette with her own' are seen several times, which 'at once captures a sanctioned mode of touching, a woman's appropriation of a male gesture, a phallic symbol, and a means of materializing sexual tension in the form of smoke or fire'. In these photographs, the women appear like kin. Moreover, these photographs, as 'tangible evidence of queer life', are circulated among private collectors and passed on to generations, and therefore, among them, 'establish connections similar to the ones they represented' (307).

Freeman's take on practical kinship and non-reproductive corporeal transfer applies to queer belonging experienced in Takarazuka and the Poe clan, where mimetic bodies are reproduced in non-procreative ways. The Poe clan shares the blood, but the way their bodies become similar to each other is not through genes but through learned behaviours. They learn to behave like humans. For example, like other vampires before or after him, Edgar is trained to show his reflection in a mirror, to appear to breathe, pulsate, and feel pain so that he can pass as a human. Moreover, the visual depictions of Edgar and Alan are similar, both in the original manga and in the Takarazuka staging. In the manga, they are mainly distinguished by their eyebrows and hairstyles with Edgar having thicker eyebrows and curly hair, while Alan has thinner eyebrows and straight hair. However, on the black-and-white pages of manga, their hair and clothing are often not shaded to be different colours, so it can sometimes be difficult to identify the characters without reading the text. In Takarazuka, they also appear similar except that Edgar has darker curly hair, while Alan has straight blond hair (see Figure 3). They wear nineteenth-century country-aristocrat outfits with a knee-length coat, a waistcoat, a frilly blouse, a loosely knotted bow tie, and knee-high boots. In the school scenes, they wear the same uniforms. In the scene where Edgar turns Alan into a vampire, they are in similar silk puff-sleeve blouses and trousers with only slight colour differences. Also, both of them wear blue eyeshadow and blue-green colour contact lenses.[30] These visual similarities, combined with Takarazuka's two-dimensional performance aesthetics, create a family resemblance between these two characters.

In *shōnen-ai* manga, as in *The Poe Clan*, visual similarity is deployed to express same-sex intimacy between two boys. In her analyses of another *shōnen-ai* manga by Hagio, *The Heart of Thomas* (*Tōma no shinzō*) (1974), Ubukata Tomoko (2009: 254) reworks Lacanian psychoanalysis to consider the sameness of boys as a visual representation of their resistance to leaving the imaginary (where children do not distinguish themselves from others) in order to stay immune to the violence of the heteronormative system naturalized in the symbolic realm (operated on the network of differences). Ubukata's discussion partially explains the relationship between Edgar and Alan, both in the manga and in the Takarazuka performance. Their sameness demonstrates their immunity from heteronormative violence, but as eternal fourteen-year-old vampires, they nullify the developmental paradigm itself, as suggested by the lack of their reflections in a mirror (which is the metaphor Lacan uses to identify the imaginary stage). In this regard, they are like the lesbian vampire whose strength Case (1991: 15) identifies as 'the fact that she cannot see herself in the mirror and remains outside that door into the symbolic'. Also, resistance to the developmental paradigm is a trait of girls' aesthetics (see Section 1).

In Takarazuka's *The Poe Clan*, a sense of sameness also encompasses other characters. Boy characters in the school uniforms resemble each other, and so

---

[30] Details such as the colour of eye shadow and contact lenses are hard to detect from the auditorium, but they can be seen in stage photographs and other publicity materials that many fans purchase.

do adult characters, especially among the same gender roles, partially owing to their similar costumes. However, all these characters, regardless of their ages and genders, resemble each other in one overarching sense: they are performed by Takarasiennes, who embody the excess and two-dimensionality of the Takarazuka style. It is the company's habitus, through which it distinguishes itself from many other theatrical performances.[31] Here again, Ubukata's discussion about the sameness of 'boys' is helpful; Takarasiennes' sameness can be taken as representing a rejection of heteronormativity in the symbolic realm.[32] Of course, fans identify traits they perceive as specific to their favourite stars, but these cannot be identified as such unless they conform to the Takarazuka style. Takarasiennes thus produce and are produced by what Tyler Bradway and Elizabeth Freeman term 'kin-aesthetics', consisting of kin, kinetics, and aesthetics. As they explain, 'kinship happens simultaneously on the terrain of kinetics, or forces acting on existing mechanisms of inclusion and exclusion *and* also on aesthetics, or the principles of artistic and symbolic organization' (Bradway & Freeman 2022: 4; emphasis in original). They further explicate that '[b]inding *kin*, *kinetic*, and *aesthetic* into *kin-aesthetics* highlights how kinship and art are both, as social practices, bound up with the work of the body; they work on and through the materiality of the body' (5; emphasis in the original). Through the bodies of Takarasiennes, Takarazuka aesthetics as habitus are transferred and kinship is formed by those who share it. In *The Poe Clan*, repeated emphasis on the clan's bond draws attention to the similarity of

---

[31] Takarazuka is often parodied by those who exploit its potential to be mined as kitsch. For example, Kegawa-zoku, a troupe led by female playwright/director Emoto Junko, parodied it in a campy style in its earlier years (Anan 2011). SMAP, a hugely popular boy band (which broke up in 2016), also parodied Takarazuka in their variety show *SMAP × SMAP* (1996–2016). The members of SMAP performed the members of the fictional, all-male 'Takenozuka' Revue (Takenozuka kagekidan). Takenozuka allowed only one male-role player, and all the others were assigned a female role. In each episode, the Takenozuka members pondered what it meant to be a man in their competition for the male role, with a theme song, 'What Is Man?' (*Otokotte nani?*). The Takenozuka Revue wittily parodied gender roles within and beyond Takarazuka. It also poked fun at Takarazuka's upper-middle-class milieu; Takenozuka is an existing, working-class neighbourhood in Tokyo.

[32] In supporting Takarasiennes' sameness, it may appear as though I am homogenizing them. In one sense I am, but I am not supporting the 'homogenization of women' that underlies the pathologization of lesbians' desire 'for the same'. As Sara Ahmed (2006: 96) argues, lesbians are pathologized in the heterosexual, sexological discourses for failing to identify bodily differences, but as she explains, 'The very idea of women desiring women because of "sameness" relies on a fantasy that women are "the same"'. Ahmed further points out that such a view of homosexuals is negligent of heterosexuals' sameness – that is, 'social and familial resemblance' produced as a result of compulsory heterosexuality. She then contends that 'the very distinction of same/difference can be questioned, especially insofar as the distinction rests on differences that are presumed to be inherent to bodily form' (97). I agree with her critique of the sexological discourses on homosexuality, and I am not suggesting that the Takarasiennes' individual differences should be subsumed under the sameness of its aesthetic habitus.

Takarasiennes who embody the same aesthetics. Some aspects of the aesthetics are explicitly taught within the TMS, whose teachers include former Takarasiennes, while others are passed from seniors to juniors within each troupe.[33] Through this process, the style renews, but it does not lose its distinctive quality.

To amplify this point, note the company's signature show *The Rose of Versailles* (*Berusaiyu no bara*), which has been staged 2,188 times since 1974 as of July 2023 (Mainichi Shimbun 2023). This is a queer romance between a 'masculine' woman soldier (performed by a male-role player) and her male lover (also performed by a male-role player).[34] Since its first production, modifications have been made and various versions have been produced with focuses on different characters. However, they retain the core story, songs, choreography, and other elements of the first production. In *The Rose of Versailles*, the Takarasiennes meet across time. This is similar to drag performance, which Freeman (2007: 309) also touches on in her exploration of queer kinship. She observes that 'The wearing of a faded form of masculinity or femininity upon one's own body constitutes … the sort of transubstantial kinship. … [I]n a drag performance, the qualities of, say, David Bowie or Madonna are both "passed on" and modified.' She further discusses emotions involved in this transubstantial kinship by citing Bourdieu:

> Bourdieu … posit[s] that emotions themselves, 'those forms of interaction seemingly most amenable to description … such as sympathy, friendship, or love', are matters of synchronized morphology, or bodies that have acquired the same dispositions because they are located in the same place in the social structure. Seen in this light, drag performances seem to be a matter of not only performing but also enacting, summoning, even *willing* 'sympathy, friendship, or love' between the dead and the living who occupy rhyming abjected, or foreclosed places in a social structure. (309; emphasis in original)

Likewise, female queer kinship in Takarazuka has been cherished with 'sympathy, friendship, or love' for more than 100 years. As a matter of fact, the management recruited male performers several times from 1919 to 1952, but each time, they faced vehement criticism from Takarasiennes and fans. Male performers were given only minor parts such as the backstage chorus, and since 1952, no effort has been made to recruit men to the company (Tsuji

---

[33] Various kinds of training that seniors give to juniors can be seen in Longinotto and Williams' film *Dream Girls* (1994). Also, Umehara Riko and Otohara Ai's *Takarazuka for Beginners* (1994) provides information about the relationships between seniors and juniors.

[34] It is a rare production in which a woman is a protagonist, but she is performed by a male-role player. For a discussion about one of the productions of *The Rose of Versailles* and the original manga, see Anan (2016; 2017).

2004: 28–85).[35] As Kawasaki Kenko (2022: 252) notes, what fans want to see on the Takarazuka stage is not men but male-role players and their interactions with female-role players and with other male-role players.

The peculiarity of the habitus that produces queer kinship in Takarazuka was highlighted when in 2021 *The Poe Clan* was revived by Koike at Umeda Arts Theater (Umeda geijutsu gekijō) in Osaka, Tokyo International Forum (Tokyo kokusai fōramu) and Misonoza in Nagoya. It was produced by Umeda Arts Theater, which is part of the Hankyu group, but not for Takarazuka.[36] Working in and outside of Takarazuka, Koike will often direct the same musical for Takarazuka and other venues. He casts a few former Takarasiennes in each of his shows outside the company, and for this production, he again cast Asumi in the role of Edgar. She had retired from the company in 2019, and had already started her career as an 'actress'. However, given her success in the Takarazuka adaptation, it must have been difficult to cast or imagine another actor in this role. Except for Asumi's Edgar, characters' genders and performers' gendered bodies were aligned. Female characters were performed by former female-role players and other women actors; male characters, including Alan, were performed by male actors. The former female-role players exhibited some Takarazuka aesthetics in their performance, but overall, they appeared 'natural' when they were with the male actors. In contrast, the performance of Edgar/Asumi differed from that of the rest of the company: it looked as though a two-dimensional being was performing among three-dimensional characters/actors. The Takarazuka aesthetics were highlighted especially when s/he was in proximity to Alan performed by Chiba Yūdai; through the excess in her performance that rejected essentialization of gendered and sexualized bodies, Asumi attempted to move towards two-dimensionality, while Chiba was simply there as a three-dimensional entity. He was a bare male body which failed to perform 'girlness' of this boy character in a *shōnen-ai* manga. The queer kinship as seen in the Takarazuka version was absent between Edgar and Alan as well as among other members of the clan.

To conclude these reflections, I return to the photographs of the mimetic bodies of lesbians that Freeman discusses. She suggests that not only is queer

---

[35] They were recruited as 'male students', like Takarasiennes as 'female students'. These male students received training within the male division. Hori Seiki and Shirai Tetsuzō, who contributed to the company in its foundation years as directors, started their careers in the male division (Tsuji 2004: 26–41). In the post-war years, the division was in operation from 1945 to 1954 (44, 131).

[36] In addition to running its theatre, Umeda Arts Theater has a management division for former Takarasiennes and Takarazuka creatives who continue working in show business. Laura MacDonald (2023) discusses the relationship of this theatre to Takarazuka in her essay on women producers of musical theatre in East Asia.

kinship seen in these photographs, but also similar connections are created among private collectors who preserve and hand them down to younger generations. Similarly, in *The Poe Clan*, such connections are established among the humans who meet Edgar and Alan, not least by framing the show's story as told by the researchers drawing on their ancestors' records, as previously described. The researchers do not see the vampires as aberrant. On the contrary, they are fascinated by these vampires who have eternal life. It is as though these human characters stand in for Takarazuka fans who are fascinated by Takarasiennes. And just as these characters are connected across time through their adoration of Edgar and Alan, so fans are connected through their love for Takarasiennes, as kin across time. These fans also 'long' to side or even 'belong' to the Takarazuka clan in a way that is similar to the fans and performers of drag that Freeman touches on, where queer intimacy can 'exceed its own time' (Freeman 2007: 299).

3 Ueda Kumiko's Experiments: De-capitalizing TAKARAZUKA

In March 2022, director Ueda Kumiko left the Takarazuka Revue after sixteen years. The departure of this 'hitmaker' (Nanashima 2023: 63) shocked fans and surprised theatregoers and critics. Ueda's works were unique in their thematic depth, and her popularity was exceptional even in the recent 'Age of Directors' (Itō 2022: 130), where mid-career and younger directors have created a diverse range of hit shows such as revues with decadently beautiful visual aesthetics, romantic musicals set in traditional Japan, and manga-inspired works. After several years being an assistant to senior directors, she made her debut in 2013 with *Prince of Tsukigumo: From the Legend of Princess Sotoori* (*Tsukigumo no miko: Sotoori hime densetsu yori*).[37] This musical, set in ancient Japan, considers history as a story told by the rulers to legitimate their rule. It was going to be staged only in the smaller Bow Hall in Takarazuka City, but the management urgently decided to run it also in Tokyo in response to an avid request from fans. Takarazuka fans are thought to be more focused on the performance of top stars rather than the stories, but the demand for this musical shows that they also appreciate works with thematic depth. Ueda's works were also recognized outside the company with prestigious awards or nominations. *People with Wings: Brahms and Clara Schumann* (*Tsubasa aru hitobito: Burāmusu to Kurara Shūman*) (2014) was nominated for the Tsuruya Nanboku Memorial Award for Drama. *One Night of Stars* (*Hoshiai hitoyo*) (2015) won the Excellent Director Award of the Yomiuri Drama Award and *Ōranki* (2021) was again nominated for the Tsuruya Nanboku Award. Her first work after departure from

---

[37] Serving as an assistant is required for all the earlier career directors in the company.

the company, *Biome* (*Baiōmu*) (2022), was nominated for the Kishida Kunio Drama Award, Japan's most prestigious award for playwrights.

Ueda does not reveal much about why she left Takarazuka. In an interview with journalist Kiyono Yumi (2023: 49–50), she says, 'You only have one reason for marriage but a lot for divorce' and only identifies Takarazuka's star system as what suffocated her. In another interview with journalist Iizuka Tomoko (2022: 12), she reflects that audiences are drawn only to the allure of gender-bending performance and not to the contents of the plays. She says she wants to create 'works that [she] found difficult to stage in Takarazuka' – that is, 'works that present new values and perspectives' (14). She was dissatisfied with entertainment theatre, and in her interview with journalist Yoshida Junko (2023: 3), she compares it to 'bread and circuses utilized by those in power' to divert the public's attention from politics. She explains, 'Too many people are unconscious of the fact that they are incited to laugh, be moved, and cry.' Given these statements, one may wonder why she entered Takarazuka. She mentions that she did not have a particular interest in the company when she applied for jobs in the creative industry to get out of routine office work, and it was the only place that offered her a position (Iizuka 2022: 11; Kiyono 2023: 50).

Ueda's post-Takarazuka works are indeed experimental and explicitly political. *Biome* portrays the interconnected nature between humans and plants. In 2023, she directed her first opera; she changed the Italian village settings of *Cavalleria rusticana* and *Pagliacci* to a working-class neighbourhood in contemporary Osaka and dealt with issues such as the fear of exclusion from social groups. She also experimented with the form by juxtaposing opera singers and contemporary dancers. These post-Takarazuka works expanded on the experiments that she started at Takarazuka. In contrast to many other directors, she brought various real-world concerns, political and economic, into the fantasy world of Takarazuka. She also parodied the conventions of Takarazuka performance. But this was all done in a way that appealed to the fans, thus granting her the power to push the boundaries of Takarazuka productions. Her fans were mesmerized and thrilled by her intelligent, playful, and passionate approach, showing that they are not always duped by bread and circuses.

To understand the appeal of Ueda's experiments, this section focuses on her critique of the capitalist exploitation of women by discussing two of her works. In the first show, *BADDY: A Rogue from the Moon* (*BADDY: Yatsu wa tsuki kara yattekuru*) (2018), she critiques the masculinist apparatus of the company that commodifies Takarasiennes' sexuality without fully acknowledging their contribution. In the second work, *Ōranki* (2021), she offers a glimpse of an anti-capitalist space, or a shared commons, which is created through the queer bodies of Takarasiennes.

3.1 *BADDY*: Is Heaven Not a Place on Earth?

BADDY: A Rogue from the Moon, performed by the Moon Troupe, is the only revue show that Ueda wrote and directed for the company. Unlike typical revue shows, which are collections of dance-and-song sequences, it is closer to a musical with a single storyline centred around a science-fiction romance between a male roguish criminal called Baddy (played by the top star Tamaki Ryō) and a female police investigator called Goody (played by the top female-role player Manaki Reika) (see Figure 4). While most of Ueda's musicals are tragic, this revue is playfully satiric, absurd, and punctuated by episodes of calculated silliness. Takarazuka productions *can be seen* as camp, but *BADDY is* camp.

BADDY is set on the Peaceful Planet Earth, which is a fictional planet-nation that has united all the countries on the earth. The planet is ruled by the Queen (played by Tōka Yurino) in a Western-style dress typical of Takarazuka's costume plays set in the nostalgic West. Not a single crime has been committed in this planet-nation since its establishment, owing to the work of the police led by female investigator Goody. As proudly sung by the Queen, Goody, and other inhabitants, with a range of prohibitions from 'smoking and drinking' to 'nuclear families and nuclear wars' (Ueda 2018b: 3), the citizens' goal is to go to heaven after death as a reward for complying with the rules of 'goodness'.[38] When the planet-nation was founded, Baddy felt suffocated and left for the moon. However, bored on the moon, this 'number one rogue in the universe' (4) returns to earth with his gang to do all sorts of wrongs. The story unfolds through a titillating romance between Baddy and Goody, who cannot resist being attracted to each other.

The Peaceful Planet Earth is clearly a parody of the Takarazuka Revue, which is famous for its many rules, as represented by the violet code, that control Takarasiennes. This is highlighted by the name of the planet-nation's capital: TAKARAZUKA CITY, written in English capital letters. In reality, the Takarazuka Revue is located in Takarazuka City, which is normally written with Chinese characters (宝塚市). TAKARAZUKA CITY was established 103 years ago, like the Takarazuka Revue.[39] In the roundtable talk with Ueda and members of the Moon Troupe, Manaki asked if Goody was more than 103 years old, and Ueda said that she was probably about 200 (Ueda & Members of the Moon Troupe 2018: 75), which conjures up the image of Takarasiennes as

---

[38] Takarazuka does not publish scripts of revue shows because usually there are almost no lines in them. I quote the lyrics from the booklet that comes with the CD compiling the numbers in this show, but the lines are from the DVD.

[39] The show opened in February 2018, when the Takarazuka Revue was 104 years old. However, it is likely that Ueda wrote the script in 2017, when the company was 103 years old.

Figure 4 Baddy and Goody on the cover of *Le CINQ* vol. 190 (2018) (Right: Manaki Reika as Goody. Left: Tamaki Ryō as Baddy (photo taken by the author).

eternal 'fairies who sell dreams'. In addition to the characters' ages, this show is filled with nonsense, such as police officers in an undercover operation at a seafood restaurant disguised as sea creatures with huge headgears of lobsters, spoiling Takarasiennes' beauty and grace, and the first 'crime' committed on the earth by Baddy, the 'number one rogue in the universe', is smoking. Peppered with such campy nonsense, the show mocks the controlling nature of the Takarazuka Revue.

Importantly, Ueda's critique also foregrounds real-world economic features of Takarazuka. In the story, the Queen decides to deposit all the planet's budget into a bank called Big Theatre Bank after making a secret deal with it. The name of the bank, Big Theatre Bank, reminds the audience of the close relationship that

Takarazuka has with Ikeda Senshū Bank, which was established with Takarazuka's founder Kobayashi Ichizō as an advisor. Takarasiennes appear in publicity for this bank, and it attracts customers by offering lottery tickets for the company's shows. In performance, at a ball hosted by Big Theatre Bank, the Queen sings, 'Money is the best lawyer' in both 'hell' and 'heaven'. The president of the bank (played by Takasumi Hayato) also sings, 'In the peaceful world, money is everything. If we work together, we can have everything at our will' (Ueda 2018b: 11). This gestures to the greed of the capitalist class that underlies the cheerful surface of TAKARAZUKA CITY on the Peaceful Planet. In the production's programme, Ueda writes that the show is a reaction to the time when 'the grey is pushed aside and we are forced to live in the narrow realm of the white' (Ueda 2018a: 5). In the aforementioned round-table talk, she also states that the Peaceful Planet Earth represents this narrow realm of the white (Ueda & Members of the Moon Troupe 2018: 80). She does not mention capitalism on these occasions, but the exchanges between the Queen and the president of the bank demonstrate the capitalist force that produces a single mode of being in the white, sanitized, gentrified realm by silencing those who do not conform to their ethos. 'Goodness' enforced on this planet turns out to be docility with the capitalist class. It is indeed surprising that Ueda was able to stage such a direct criticism of Takarazuka. I assume that Ueda's popularity and the expectation of the show's economic success underpinned the management's decision to present it. Thus, as in the show, greed also wins in real life. Ueda must have been keenly aware of this, but she continued producing critical works, including *Ōranki* (2021), up until her retirement.

3.2 The Watchword Is 'Shine': How Takarasiennes Work

BADDY critiques the capitalist exploitation of women in Takarazuka and beyond, but to discuss this requires background information on the working conditions of Takarasiennes engaged in what Angela McRobbie (2016: 74) terms 'passionate work'. As she details, creative industries incite and exploit the passion of individuals who willingly offer themselves to temporary-based, low-paid jobs with long working hours as a default to feel emotionally rewarded for being approved as entrepreneurial, creative individuals. Many Takarasiennes were Takarazuka fans themselves and to achieve their dream job of being a Takarasienne, they invested so much of their time and effort (as well as their families' money) in preparation by taking lessons in performing arts to pass through the extremely narrow gate of the TMS. To maintain this job, they willingly and passionately exhaust themselves through the arduous labour that performing as a Takarasienne demands. McRobbie further points out that passionate work is often gendered female, typically motivated by naïve enthusiasm, which is part of 'normative femininity'

(110). Indeed, 'normative femininity' is cherished in Takarazuka (see Section 1), where passionate workers are preyed on. In the Takarazuka empire, the creation of such workers begins at the TMS. McRobbie observes that in the UK, the development of the entrepreneurial mindset and skills, or 'the development of human capital', is now part of the school curriculum (67). The same obtains for Takarazuka in Japan. As early as 1919, the TMS was established to invest in students/artists as human capital. Its graduates, or Takarasiennes as passionate human capital, generate daily ticket sales of more than JPY 30,000,000 (GBP 154,700 as of December 2024) (Nakamoto 2011: 204), which is worth the monthly salary of 300 junior Takarasiennes.[40]

While Takarasiennes' labour is exploited, other female workers in the company are often marginalized or simply non-existent. For instance, note how in Takarazuka's long history, *BADDY* is the first revue show directed by a woman. The first female musical director was Ueda Keiko, who was hired as late as 1993.[41] In recent years, more female directors have been appointed, but as of 2023, only six out of twenty-eight are women.[42] What is also surprising is that there have been neither female producers nor female heads of the production department (Tabe & Kawai 2024: 26). Ueda Kumiko was thus one of the pioneers. Tamaki Ryō, the then top star of the Moon Troupe who played Baddy, recalled that Ueda mentioned in a rehearsal that if the show failed, other female directors would not be able to follow her (Daily Sports Online 2018). Thus, *BADDY* is a collaborative attempt by Ueda and the Takarasiennes to open the way for future female directors of revue shows. It must have been a difficult task for them as the show needed to achieve two kinds of success – financial success by successfully critiquing the company.

Despite the unequal opportunities for women in the company, Takarazuka may initially seem an ideal workplace for female performers because, as an all-female company, it is a place where women occupy the stage, as symbolized by the Queen in *BADDY*. The company is also a school, where every woman is (supposed to be) treated equally as a student; if they complete the coursework at the TMS, they can all enter the company. While a hierarchy exists between seniors and juniors and between top stars and other stars, under the leadership of the top star members of each troupe strive to create good performances. The top stars' ability to lead eighty members of each troupe, as well as Takarasiennes' passionate pursuit of artistic excellence, gains respect from and potentially imbues a sense of empowerment in

---

[40] The figure is based on two productions per day at the Tokyo Takarazuka Theater (Nakamoto 2011: 204). Information about Takarasiennes' salaries is provided later in this section.
[41] She is not a relative of Ueda Kumiko.
[42] Takarazuka does not offer details of its creatives. I estimated the number of directors from the January 2023 issue of *Opera* (*Kageki*), where their New Year's greetings are printed.

their female spectators, many of whom are also working women (Nakamoto 2011: 188–214). Stars in Takarazuka shine and women in their audiences may also feel encouraged by them to shine.

The word 'shine' (*kagayaku*) is often used to describe Takarasiennes' allure in various media, and it is also the keyword of a neoliberal economic policy for women implemented by the Japanese government. For instance, in 2014 under the leadership of the late prime minister Abe Shinzō, it established the Headquarters to Create a Society in Which Every Woman Shines (Subete no josei ga kagayaku shakai zukuri honbu), to accelerate women's entry into the labour market. In 2015, the Act for the Promotion of Women's Participation and Advancement in the Workplace (Josei katsuyaku suishin hō) became law, and in 2016, the scope of the act was expanded to include the elderly (with the aim to reduce social welfare such as pension and insurance): the Cabinet passed the plan to promote the Dynamic Engagement of All Citizens (Ichioku sōkatsuyaku). Nonetheless, women's ability/power (*chikara*) continues to be identified as the largest unused potential of Japan (Gender Equality Bureau Cabinet Office 2016). Thus, to shine is to work – work for productive, waged labour, taking no account of unwaged, reproductive labour (Katada 2021: 20) in which women have traditionally been engaged, such as caring not only for children and the elderly but also for men as the waged, productive labour force.

Takarasiennes shine not only as stars but also as working women in a neoliberal Japan. Moreover, they are 'winners' – those who won one of the competitive, limited places in the TMS and the company. The income of junior members is reported to be about JPY 100,000–130,000 per month after deduction of dorm rent, etcetera (GBP 516–670 as of December 2024) (FNN Prime Online 2023).[43] This is much less than the average annual salary in Japan, which is JPY 4,600,000 as of 2023 (GBP 23,720 as of December 2024) (National Tax Agency 2024), but considering their age (late teens to twenties), their salaries after deduction are not particularly meagre, although not commensurate with their highly physical labour that extends into the evening. In any case, the amount of their salaries may not be a major issue for them; they are mostly from wealthy families able to support their work in performing arts (Kawasaki 2005: 168). Moreover, the company guarantees them full-time employment for the first five years (Fujii & Tanaka 2023). This is quite different from the environment of other creatives typically working as freelancers.

---

[43] Takarazuka does not disclose its employees' salaries. The information about junior members' salaries and working conditions was leaked to the media.

However, at the end of their fifth year, Takarasiennes' contracts are switched to a freelance-based arrangement (Fujii & Tanaka 2023).[44] Under Japanese law, if a fixed-term contract is renewed for a total of five years at the same workplace, an employee has the right to convert to permanent employment. Takarazuka's freelance system evades this law. If the company gave permanent contracts to Takarasiennes, their number would increase and it would have to radically change the current system of operating with five troupes. It would also become difficult to continue the rule of retirement upon marriage. Also, it should be noted that by ending full-time contracts, the company is no longer obliged to contribute to employees' welfare, such as pensions and health insurance. Despite all of this, the management states that the freelance system is for Takarasiennes to 'improve their skills within their own time' (Fujii & Tanaka 2023). This wording suggests that freelance Takarasiennes have commitments other than their work for Takarazuka. However, although they should be able to have control over how they work as freelancers, they remain under the control of the management. As before, they must perform in one to two productions per day (each consisting of a musical and a revue) in Takarazuka and Tokyo, each of which runs for a month and a half, and in addition, they also perform at other venues and appear in various media. Furthermore, unlike other freelance creatives, they cannot work in different companies without the permission of the management. Even with this possibility, it has been reported that no freelance Takarasiennes have tried to have contracts with other agents since joining the company (Fujii & Tanaka 2023); to reiterate, being a Takarasienne, rather than an actor, is their dream job. Also, they still need to obey the violet code. Given the control the company has over most aspects of the Takarasiennes' lives, it is possible to force them to devote most of their time to the company. As a former Takarasienne, Higashi Koyuki, recalls, it is not unusual for Takarasiennes not to have time for what is essential for living, such as 'meals, sleep, and bath' (Matsumuro & Seki 2023: 3). The stress of the working conditions in Takarazuka only became public when a member of the Cosmos Troupe committed suicide in September 2023 due to overwork and bullying by other troupe members (see Postscript).

Earlier in the company's history, protection from overexploitation was provided by the Takarazuka labour union. It was established in 1946 with Sudō Gorō, a conductor of the orchestra and a composer, as the chairperson. Amatsu Otome and Kasugano Yachiyo, two superstars in the earlier years, served as vice-chairpersons (Matsumuro 2024: 1). The union won better working conditions such as not allowing work after 10:00 p.m., as recalled by a former

---

[44] This will change to a one-year fixed term but renewable contract in March 2025. See Postscript for details. The discussion in this section is based on the system before March 2025.

Takarasienne, Tamai Hamako (1999: 98). However, it disbanded after the freelance system was implemented in 1977, in which Takarasiennes were rehired as freelancers from their eighth year in the company (Matsumuro 2024: 1). The weaker status of freelancers in Japan renders it hard to continue organized labour movements (Morisaki cited in Matsumuro 2024: 1). In the current system, the freelance contracts start in their sixth year, making their status even more vulnerable. This means that the 'euphoria and excitement' (McRobbie 2016: 79) of engaging in their dream jobs may not always last. The overall number of Takarasiennes remains at 400, while 40 new members join yearly, meaning 40 leave yearly. They do not make the reasons public – their 'graduation' appears as a natural course of their 'studentship'. However, it is likely that the freelance system is used to screen them – those who were not offered good conditions by the company when converting into freelancers are likely to leave (Sakabe 2020: 200). Most performers are in their late twenties to mid thirties when they retire, still having a long way to go in their lives.[45] Some pursue successful careers in show business, while others 'disappear'. Among the latter, there are those making careers in other fields, but one might speculate that they encounter difficulties after devoting much of their lives – and passion – to their roles/occupations as Takarasiennes. It is telling that Mizu Natsuki, a former top star of the Snow Troupe, when asked what she wanted to do after her retirement in 2010, said: 'I want to learn more about society [outside Takarazuka]' (Nakamoto 2011: 207). This comment exhibits Takarasiennes' naiveté about the world at large, produced by and maintained in the company.

3.3 'Yell for All the Women Who Have Been Suppressed'

Against the backdrop of these working conditions at Takarazuka, *BADDY* protests the company's capitalist exploitation of Takarasiennes in two ways: by making the non-normative sexual appeal of the company explicit and by staging a performance of female anger. As discussed in Sections 1 and 2, the company commodifies non-normative sexual glamour performed by women while rendering the possibility of homosexual (not homosocial) intimacy non-existent in the sphere of the 'nickname existence' (Azuma 2015). Furthermore, onstage, it either limits homosexuality to side characters (with a few exceptions such as *The Poe Clan* and *Nijinsky*) or only includes brief homoerotic scenes without clear storylines in revue shows.[46] In other words, the company feeds off

---

[45] As mentioned in Section 1, Takarasiennes do not disclose their ages during their tenure at the company. I was able to find or estimate their ages because those who pursue their acting careers outside the company after retirement often make their ages public.

[46] However, it should be remembered that the Takarazuka production of *The Poe Clan* does not clearly identify Edgar and Alan as homosexuals.

(female) queer intimacy while marginalizing queerness. By contrast, *BADDY* foregrounds it. Baddy is attracted to Goody, but he is also romantically involved with a character named Sweetheart, a member of his gang, who does not have a fixed gender identity. Performed by a male-role player, Miya Rurika, Sweetheart may be 'biologically male' but mixes both male and female speech styles in a tone of voice that falls somewhere between male and female characters.[47] Sweetheart also wears both male and female costumes. Such a way of being and loving does not exist in TAKARAZUKA CITY, and therefore seeing Baddy and Sweetheart dancing intimately confuses Goody and her colleague Pocky (played by Tsukishiro Kanato): 'He is a man/ He is a man, too/ Woman?/ We don't know/ We don't know/ Why?/ Why?' (Ueda 2018b: 5). At the sight of their kiss, Goody and Pocky scream and faint. The non-existence of queer love in this city allegorizes the pretence of the management. Moreover, Goody and Pocky's inability to process Sweetheart's gender fluidity is a dig at the company, as it specializes in and *capitalizes* on the presentation of furtive queer love on stage.

While the romance between Baddy and Sweetheart makes explicit the queer intimacy that the company sells, the show also includes a song-and-dance sequence that can be seen as an expression of Takarasiennes' anger at their exploitation. Titled 'Goody's Anger' (*Guddi no ikari*), this sequence follows the robbery of the planet's budget at Big Theatre Bank committed by Baddy and his gang. (This may be symbolic in that Takarasiennes take back the money earned from their exploitation.) Although Goody was at the site of the robbery, her crush on Baddy clouded her judgement and she was unable to prevent the crime. She explodes with anger towards him. Wiping off the smile she always wore as a sign of 'normative femininity', she sings:

> He has ruined everything/ Where has the peace of this planet gone?/ He has made a mess of everything/ He has changed everything/ I won't forgive him, I can't forgive him/ I will never allow anyone to overthrow my beliefs/ I've never known emotions like this/ I'm angry. I'm angry. I'm alive. Now. (Ueda 2018b: 11)

---

[47] Miya retired in 2019. Coincidentally, they have been working ever since as what they call a 'gender-free artist', meaning an artist who does not have a fixed gender, unlike other male-role players who 'become actresses'. Miya says in an interview that they were able to make this decision because of the social situation around the time they retired when the public interest in gender issues was increasing. They recall that it would have been much more difficult to do this if their retirement had been just a few years earlier. The information is from Glitter_channel (2021) www.youtube.com/watch?v=vX90xvZN6Ac (accessed 2 September 2024). They do not specify #Me Too as part of their source of inspiration, but I assume that it probably was.

This expression of 'Goody's Anger' also resounds with the collective anger of Takarasiennes at being exploited as passionate workers performing normative femininity as Goodies, a group of female junior police officers, join her to perform the Rockette dance. The Rockette is always performed in the company's revue shows by younger Takarasiennes to showcase their prettiness, youthful eroticism, and well-trained bodies that move in unison. In *BADDY*, the prettiness in unison is transformed into a powerful roar in solidarity as they sing together, 'We are now alive/ We are angry/ We are crying/ We are shedding tears' (12). Some other female characters, even the Queen, appear on stage and join Goody and Goodies, creating a larger collective 'We'. At this point, the target of their anger is clearly 'something bigger' than Baddy, going beyond the story of the show. They repeatedly sing, 'won't allow!' (*yurusanai!*) (12). The Japanese language allows the omission of a subject and an object of a verb if they are apparent from the context, and this invites the audience to interpret the subject of 'won't allow' as all of the Takarasiennes and the object as the exploitation of Takarasiennes by the company. The sequence starts with the performance of Goody's anger at Baddy, who stole the planet's budget, but it turns into the manifestation of women's collective anger at their labour being stolen by the capitalist force.

In her analysis of this 'angry Rockette' sequence, Kiyono (2023: 49) focuses on the gender hierarchy within Takarasiennes and argues that the scene symbolizes the revolt of female-role players subordinated to male-role players. One exception to this hierarchy was the female-role player who played Goody, Manaki Reika, whose popularity was equivalent to male-role players. Hence critic Tsuruoka Eriko (2018: 9) writes that Manaki 'showed that, after 100 years of Takarazuka, a new style of the top pair has become possible where a female-role player can be on the same footing with a male-role player without subordinating herself to the male-role player'. Manaki is one of only three female-role players for whom the company produced shows where they performed starring roles.[48] However, their shows were at the smaller Bow Hall, not the Takarazuka Grand Theater. Also, their male-role partners were not in the same shows and therefore they were not shown as being on the same footing as their male-role counterparts. In light of this, the 'angry Rockette' can be seen as a protest against such treatment. Nonetheless, it is important to point out that Rockette dancers in Takarazuka include male-

---

[48] The other two are Kazahana Mai (who performed in the company from 1990 to 1999) and Tsukikage Hitomi (1990–2002). However, before the top star system in which a male-role player is appointed as the top of each troupe was consolidated in the 1970s (a female top star is the 'sub' top), the company produced works with female protagonists performed by female-role players (Nakamoto 2011: 156–157).

role players. In *BADDY*, seven out of twenty-one Goodies/Rockettes are male-role players. (When performing the Rockette, they perform as women in female costumes.) Therefore the anger that Ueda stages is not only female-role players' but also Takarasiennes', regardless of their gender roles. Moreover, in a wider context, it also expresses female anger at their treatment within the masculinist social/economic structure.

This production opened in February 2018, just a few months after #Me Too went viral. Although Ueda did not make any comment on the movement, as Kiyono (2023: 49) observes, it is difficult not to see the production in this context. Elaine Aston (2020: 63) discusses '#Me Too as disobedient speech endowed with a capacity to ignite attachments to anti-patriarchal sentiments'. Drawing on Tony Fisher's articulation of dissensual speech, Aston elaborates on the phatic and agonic dimensions of 'me too'/#Me Too. It is phatic because the utterance 'me too' demonstrates the establishment of the equal relationship between 'I' and another 'I' sharing something in common, or a 'grievance' (Fisher cited in Aston 2020: 63) over injustice. It is agonic in that it brings whoever with the same political concern into collective existence. In sum, writes Aston, through phatic and agonic dimensions of 'me too', a collective of those who rebel against patriarchy comes into being (63). To these two dimensions, she adds an affective dimension as an indispensable drive that makes 'me too'/#Me Too a dissensual speech: it 'repeats ad infinitum *ressentiment* against male abuse of power' (64; emphasis in original). She explains:

> [P]hatic/agonic contestation of patriarchy is motivated by *feelings* of injustice and the *longing* for a more equitable social order. Unlike the individualistic 'I' who believes she has the freedom to choose, the woman who identifies with #Me Too realises the power of patriarchy to injure. As the feeling-voicing of injury multiplies, the woman who declares 'me too' becomes one of the many – a disobedient, collectivist subject who dissents from the unspoken 'law' of male supremacy. (64; emphasis in original)

Theatre is a medium through which performers, audiences, playwrights, directors, and many others involved share their individual feeling-voicing, thus generating a *collective* feeling-voicing. Audiences witness the anger of Goody and Goodies as their own and express their affective reactions on social media with words such as 'moving',[49] 'boiling',[50] 'empowered',[51] and 'I shed

---

[49] *furuzukka 24 jikan Takarazuka* [Full-zukka: Twenty-four Hours of Takarazuka] (2020). https://ameblo.jp/furuzukka/entry-12600813710.html (accessed 20 November 2024).

[50] *2828☆Takarazuka fuan* [2828☆Takarazuka fan] (2018). http://blog.livedoor.jp/golden_kagalin/archives/29637590.html (accessed 20 November 2024).

[51] *furuzukka 24 jikan Takarazuka*.

tears'.⁵² Exploitation of women's labour is certainly not limited to Takarazuka. The government urges women's entry into the labour market, but they are not treated equally to male workers. This is most clearly exhibited in the wage gap; as of 2024, the standard wage for women in Japan is between 70 and 80 per cent of men's (Miyawaki & Okabayashi 2024), showing that women are needed primarily as cheaper labour.

'[F]eelings of injustice and the longing for a more equitable social order' flow from the Takarasiennes' bodies performing the Rockette. Choreographed by Miori Yumino, a former female-role player serving as an in-house choreographer, the women raise their fists, wildly kick up their legs while keeping them apart so that their bodies remain steady and grounded. All of these are uncommon movements for female characters, especially for Rockettes. Ueda's lyrics and music by Aoki Asako, a female composer of the company, create moments when the women are almost rapping, as though their anger, energy, and exultation cannot be contained within the melody played by the Takarazuka orchestra. The word in the lyrics that stands out is 'activation' (*kasseika*) (Ueda 2018b: 12). They repeat it many times at a fast pace triumphantly as if they urge themselves – and the audience – to activate themselves, or to wake themselves up, to think and act for themselves. As a scientific term, 'activation' is an unusual word to be used in Takarazuka's lyrics, and it made a strong impression on the audience; many fans wrote about it on social media. Another unexpected phrase coming from these women is 'Hear us roar (*kono sakebi kikeyo*)' (12), resonating with women's movements including #Me Too. Japanese speech patterns are often gender specific, and in the original Japanese lyrics, Ueda adopts a masculine pattern of the imperative form of the verb 'hear', which is *kikeyo*. This is a demand, not a request, to be heard, which men can 'naturally' utter, demonstrating in turn how unusual it is for women to demand to be heard. Normally, women would use a request form, *kiite*. Therefore *kikeyo*, shouted by the Rockettes, who are usually the embodiment of prettiness, is extremely invigorating. They shout that patriarchy injures them, to borrow Aston's phrase. They declare that they turn the blood they bleed as a drive to activate themselves, as they sing, 'I feel my blood/ Rushing through my body' (11) and 'I have recalled/ Blood-coloured/ Life/ Give it back to me' (12).

The Rockette sequence ends with the women's kick line as they sing: 'Anger/ Sorrow/ Burning/ Here is my life/ in order to fight for myself/ in order to fight for my own/ Rising up/ Now I am/ ... I'm alive now/ I'm alive' (12).⁵³ Earlier,

---

⁵² *Jinsei de hitsuyō na chie wa subete Takarazuka kara mananda* [Everything I Need to Know in My Life, I Learned It from Takarazuka] (2018). http://mutsugoro.cocolog-nifty.com/butsubutsu/2018/04/post-ed91.html (accessed 20 November 2024).

⁵³ The lyrics, 'in order to fight for myself/ in order to fight for my own', are originally written in English. It is common to have English phrases in Japanese popular songs.

I pointed out the irony that Takarasiennes as passionate labourers empower female audience members. However, at the end of this Rockette sequence, they must have been empowered in a different way, fuelling their anger with the 'longing for a more equitable social order' ignited by the Rockettes; a fan commented in her blog that this sequence was a 'yell for all the women who have been suppressed'.[54]

In the end, both Baddy and Goody die. Pocky explodes Baddy's base so that Goody can get in to arrest him, but they die together in the fire following the explosion. Before their deaths, the tension between love and hostility unfolds in a dance duet. (A partnered dance by the top pair is always included in the company's revue shows.) Towards the end of the scene, Baddy tells Goody to escape, but she chooses to stay with him. They kiss for the first and last time. This dramatic, emotional scene is straightforwardly Takarazuka-like, demonstrating Ueda's ability to create what is typical while often subverting it. This scene is followed by the finale, the hallmark of the company, where Takarasiennes come down the huge stairs as they sing numbers from the show. They usually remove the 'masks' of characters and sing as Takarasiennes. However, in *BADDY*, the story continues into the finale. In its opening, the death of Baddy and Goody is announced by the police officers, who conclude their announcement: 'Peace has returned to the earth. This is the Peaceful Planet here. People live without any problems and they will go to heaven.' It sounds as though Ueda is saying, 'I know. Just one show like this can't change the Takarazuka apparatus.'

Nonetheless, Ueda quickly overturns this pessimism. As characters come down the stairs, it becomes clear that the setting of the finale is moved from earth to heaven, where they, including Baddy and his gang, reside. Thus heaven is not what the inhabitants of the Peaceful Planet Earth are told. It is where everyone ends up. This subversion is expressed in the lyrics of the final number, 'Peaceful Paradise'.[55] It is a collection of a few numbers in this show, but the lyrics are slightly altered. For example, it opens with the lyrics sung earlier in the show, 'Peaceful Planet/ Peaceful Planet' but adds, 'Someday/ Goodbye' (Ueda 2018b: 14). Also, although Goody sang earlier, 'Love is beautiful/ Let the flower of love bloom all over the world' (14), she sings in the finale, 'Flower of love doesn't always bloom/ But in such a world/ Let's walk together someday/ Dream of you and me/ In such a world, let's love each other' (14). Walking together and loving each other are possible only when the parties involved *hear* each other. The lyrics are charged with the wish that such an environment will

---

[54] *Jinsei de hitsuyō na chie wa subete Takarazuka kara mananda.*
[55] The original title is in English.

be created within and beyond Takarazuka. Moreover, since love (*ai*) and dream (*yume*) are the two catchphrases of the company, Ueda may be asking if the management truly cares about these. The show ends with Baddy singing along with all the characters. Earlier, he sang alone: 'Get out of my way!/ No one can stop me/ I'm atrocious/ Don't stop me, I am BAD!/ I'm BADDY!/ ... / Be Free!' (4) but this time, he sings with everyone: 'Get out of my way!/ No one can stop me/ Don't waste your breath/ Don't stop me, I am BAD!/ I'm BADDY!/ ... / Be Free!' (4).[56] Here, female characters sing with male characters by using the male first-person pronoun *ore* and male speech style. They also *demand* obstacles to get out of their way, echoing the angry Rockettes. As the finale crescendos, the characters perform all sorts of un-Takarazuka behaviours. Baddy and Sweetheart blow each other a kiss, and Sweetheart and Pocky perform a gesture of kissing by facing each other and pouting their lips. Moreover, all the characters smoke (nonsensically huge fake cigarettes). Baddy and Goody even share a flame by touching each other's cigarette, reminiscent of the lesbians in the photographs mentioned in Section 2. What was prohibited on Peaceful Planet Earth is possible in heaven – a heaven momentarily glimpsed on the Takarazuka stage, but a heaven that can linger on in fans' memories of the performance.

3.4 Ōranki: Stream of Care

BADDY ends with a glimpse of heaven for all, and this anticipates the theme of unification in *Ōranki* (2021), Ueda's last work for Takarazuka, also performed by the Moon Troupe. Unlike campy *BADDY*, *Ōranki* is a serious musical based on the history of the Nanboku-chō Period (1336–1392), when Japan was split into two courts with two emperors. Originally, the emperor and the aristocracy were in the imperial court in Kyoto, but a military leader called the shōgun drove them away and they ended up in Nara. The shōgun created a rival imperial court in Kyoto and installed a puppet emperor. Since Kyoto is north of Nara, the court in Kyoto was referred to as the northern court and the court in Nara as the southern court. The protagonist is a samurai named Kusunoki Masatsura (played by Tamaki Ryō) who fights for the south. The story centres on his internal conflict about fighting losing battles in the face of the north's overwhelming force of arms. He proposes to the southern emperor that they negotiate peace with the north to allow the south to survive. However, his proposal is dismissed as the emperor and aristocrats are too proud. Deeply frustrated by this rejection, Masatsura questions his loyalty to the losing south as he does not have his own reason for fighting for the south.

---

[56] The lyrics 'Don't stop me, I am BAD!/ I'm BADDY!/ ... / Be Free!' are originally in English.

Rather, his loyalty is based on his dead father's loyalty to the south. Later, the shōgun tries to recruit him to the north, and in rejecting him, Masatsura discovers a reason to fight for the south, namely the creation of a unified country. Ueda coined the title *Ōranki*, which is a novel combination of Chinese characters for 'cherry blossoms', 'storm', and 'story'. In Japan, cherry blossoms symbolize fleeting beauty, and as the southern court was in an area famous for its cherry blossoms (Yoshino, Nara), the title suggests that the storm of war will lead to the end of the south. It also resonates with the emotional storm within Masatsura and his eventual death in the war.

Characters in this costume play are mostly historical figures. Masatsura's romance with Ben no Naishi (played by Misono Sakura), a daughter of an aristocrat in the south, is derived from *Yoshino shūi*, a collection of medieval tales.[57] However, Ueda drew on this historical material to fashion a contemporary critique of capitalism. She did not discuss capitalism in relation to *BADDY*, but did so in her discussion with members of the Moon Troupe engaged for the production of *Ōranki*.[58] She brings a contemporary perspective to events that happened in the pre-capitalist past, arguing that samurais in the north were driven by self-centred motivation, 'similar to many in our contemporary capitalist society', where 'the pursuit of individual happiness' is the aim of life. In contrast to these samurais, she explains, she portrayed Masatsura as a character with a state of mind that drives individuals to act outside of transient personal interests and capitalist greed (Ueda & Members of the Moon Troupe 2021: 58), thereby raising the issue of care, which is a central concern of the show.

In the musical, the caring ethos of the Kusunoki community is foregrounded. The Kusunoki clan and its samurais show their gratitude to the farmers for feeding them, and the farmers are grateful for the Kusunokis' work to protect them from the northern attacks. The notion of interdependent lives is widely shared by the community and the Kusunoki people also give medical care to their enemies after battle. This is in contrast to the self-centred greed found in the northern court. Moreover, although Ueda only associates the north with

---

[57] *Yoshino shūi* is said to have been written between the fourteenth and sixteenth centuries, but the details are unclear.

[58] In her published lecture at Kyoto University, titled 'In a Dangerous Time of Bread and Circuses [*Pan to sākasu no abunai jidai ni*]', Ueda (2018c: 17–19) identifies capitalism as a force to stimulate and increase people's desires limitlessly while depriving them of an ability to think for themselves. In the published version, there is no discussion of her plays, but a fan who attended the lecture reported in her blog that Ueda showed clips from *BADDY* in relation to another key theme of the lecture, which is the mutual surveillance society. See *Yukiko no heya* [*Yukiko's Room*] (2020). https://yukiko221b.hatenablog.com/entry/2020/01/13/202857 (accessed 21 September 2024). I was not able to attend this lecture, so I do not know for certain whether or not she related *BADDY* to her criticism of capitalism.

capitalism in the discussion with the troupe members, the way she depicts the southern court also suggests its self-centred nature. In the north, the greed is represented by the shōgun's deputy, Kō no Moronao (played by Shimon Yuriya), who lies to the shōgun (Kazama Yuno) to maximize his reward. For example, when Masatsura is pushing back northern forces in a battle, Moronao could engage his troops to defeat him. Instead, he delays going into battle by pretending that he has food poisoning; his reward will be better if he wins after the other northern generals have been shown to be weak. In the south, the court nobles exploit their samurais. Since the nobles' status is higher than samurais', they are unconcerned about sacrificing their samurais in a losing war, unwilling to compromise or negotiate with the north. As the leader of the samurais of the south, Masatsura's character arc involves him struggling with the exploitation of his fellow samurais and questioning his loyalty to a side that does not care for its warriors.

The key transition point occurs when Masatsura is recruited by the north. The shōgun, who is impressed by his intelligence and war tactics, suggests Masatsura join the north and gain family fame. Moronao seconds the shōgun, saying, 'This world is driven by desires. Fame. Women. Take whatever you want!' (Ueda 2021: 55). Masatsura also recalls the southern court nobles who speak of their interests: 'The only way to go is to defeat the northern court thoroughly. Don't disgrace the honour of loyalty!' (55). (In performance, they appear on the stage and utter their lines like spectres.) Masatsura silences them:

> Shut up! No more mess of these petty things! I will use my life, which Father and Mother gave me, for what is larger. Not for family fame. Neither for greed nor for loyalty . . . . . . Is this . . . a stream? Hey, can't you see? A large stream of this country . . . I met commoners who cried, swallowed by a violent stream. I met a girl who was about to be swallowed by a grudge and devote her life to revenge. Someone needs to do something about it, before it becomes a tsunami and engulfs many. My stream runs only for several decades. But our country has a much longer stream. Lord Takauji [the name of the shōgun], I flatter myself that it is only the Kusunokis that can guide the southern court. I can't abandon it until our country becomes peaceful. (55)

The key image here is the stream. It refers to the stream of time and also the stream of life and a kind of force that affects living beings. Hence, this marks Masatsura's decision to embark on a long-term process of directing this stream in a better direction. He is aware that the south is on the verge of extinction and has decided that his destiny is to save the stream of life in the south by eventually realizing its unification with the north, despite the objections raised by the nobles. It is important that the unification Masatsura envisions does not allow the south to be colonized by the north. Neither does it mean the loss of the Kusunokis' caring culture. Unlike the united Peaceful Planet in *BADDY*, Masatsura's proposal for a unified country rests on taking care of its inhabitants and creating a livable world for all.

In her studies of care, Okano Yayo identifies home as a site of caring relationships or a site of love (with the acknowledgement that it is not always the case, and it can be a site for extreme violence). Also, unlike the liberal conception of home as a private sphere based on the 'sameness' of the inhabitants, she argues that this is the very site in which inhabitants acquire sociability through experiencing contingent encounters with others, developing and acknowledging interdependent relationships with them. The encounters are contingent, as at home we enter into relationships with others whom we did not choose ourselves (Okano 2012: 144). At home, a group of others live different temporalities with different experiences and ideas, but despite differences, or because of the differences, they struggle to learn to accept and respect each other, even when they do not always understand each other. Underlying the struggle is the celebration of each other's existence (226, 241) and acknowledgement of the interdependent nature of lives – the carers were once cared for by others (246). The unification of the country envisioned by Masatsura entails this conception of home and caring practices. Different people, those from the north and the south, as well as aristocrats, samurais, and commoners, meet and celebrate each other's existence in a home/country where care is 'streamed' to everyone. It is to the 'birth' of this home/country that Masatsura dedicates his labour.

I should note here that I am wary about the comparison of a country with home, as it risks reinforcing the chauvinistic idea of a family-state where citizens are required to be united under the patriarch by the sameness, ethnic sameness in particular. However, 'home' theorized in care studies challenges this idea: it proposes home as a place of inclusive differences. This may seem at odds with Takarazuka as a place for queer kinship marked by the mimetic bodies of Takarasiennes as discussed in Section 2. However, to reiterate: the sameness seen in an alternative, non-reproductive queer kinship is the antithesis of conservative gender and sexual ideology typically endorsed by a heteronormative family-state. Therefore, the sameness found in queer kinship is not the same as the sameness within a liberal conception of a home.

I termed Masatsura's work as 'birth' to emphasize that care work, traditionally undertaken by women (and those who have no place in the public sphere), has often been associated with motherhood. I am not claiming that care work is essentially feminine or maternal, and I am also aware that more recent scholarship in care studies does not adopt such a view (Thompson 2020: 40). Yet it should be stressed that, in this show for the Takarazuka stage, a character who challenges capitalist greed is portrayed with a 'feminine' quality, highlighting the masculinist nature of this greed. Takarasiennes' protest at the exploitation by the management staged in *BADDY* resounds in *Ōranki*. A 'feminine' Masatsura, performed by a woman, determines to create a world which is liveable for all, not based on exploitation but on the awareness of interdependent lives. A 'feminine' Masatsura mounts objection to the liberal conception of man as an autonomous self, 'a narcissist who sees the world in his own image', 'who has no awareness of the limits of his own desires and passion' (Benhabib 1987: 84) – narcissists like the samurais in the north, the court nobles in the south, and the Takarazuka management, who perceive themselves as expanding in a limitless manner in the 'other-less' world, echoing the capitalist illusion of limitless expansion. Masatsura's work of unification involves negotiation with liberal and capitalist ideals, as the catchphrase of *Ōranki* printed on the poster and flyer suggests: 'Be aware of your limit. Be aware of your life (*Kagiri o shiri inochi o shire*)' (see Figure 5).

One may wonder why *Ōranki* does not present female characters/female-role players standing up against capitalist and masculinist exploitation. Unlike in *BADDY*, female characters in *Ōranki*, even a heroine, Ben no Naishi, do not play active roles in the story. They are either victims of sexual abuse by Moronao, women obsequious to men in power, or partners of the Kusunoki brothers simply adding a romantic flavour to the story. This is because this musical follows historical incidents; it is the historical fact that Masatsura and the Kusunoki samurais, not female figures, fought the north. However, the way Ueda portrays Masatsura enables the audience to identify a 'feminine' quality in him. In Takarazuka shows where female characters cannot be protagonists, Masatsura is a device for women – both the Takarasiennes and the female audience – to mount a critique of the capitalist force.

It should also be pointed out that, although 'feminine' and 'masculine' are treated as opposites in character portrayals, the dichotomy gets disrupted when the various layers of Takarasiennes' existence are taken into account. Masatsura as a caring 'maternal' male character is performed by a male-role player who is a woman. Ueda created caring characters, both women and men, in other of her works, but a comparison of *Ōranki* with her debut musical, *Prince of Tsukigumo*, also performed by the Moon Troupe, emphasizes her queering of care in *Ōranki*, as Tamaki Ryō and Hōzuki An performed in both shows. In *Prince of Tsukigumo*, they played the roles of self-centred brothers, while caring roles were assigned to maternal characters (mother and nanny) performed by female-role players. In

Figure 5 Flyer of *Ōranki*. Right: Misono Sakura as Ben no Naishi. Middle and left: Tamaki Ryō as Kusunoki Masatsura. Lower left: Tsukishiro Kanato as Kusunoki Masanori. Right: The catchphrase, 'Be aware of your limit. Be aware of your life' (photo taken by the author).

contrast, in *Ōranki*, Tamaki and Hōzuki performed Masatsura and his brother Masatoki. This is not just a reversal of gender in care work; in *Ōranki*, care is practised by men in the story, but at other levels by women – women who perform different genders flexibly as male-role players and as female students and create a 'queer kinship' with other women. Seen in this light, care practised by male rather than female characters in *Ōranki* potentially enables spectators to imagine more clearly the notion of a queer 'home/family' as antithetical to the *care-less* capitalist empire of the company.[59]

Nonetheless, it must also be acknowledged that Masatsura's participation in the battle with the north at the end of the play is at odds with care work, even though his purpose is to push back the north to obtain a better condition for peace negotiations as the first step towards unification. His fight 'for the sake of the country' even risks appearing nationalist. Kawasaki Kenko (2024: 97) argues that *Ōranki* reinforces the Japanese mentality at the end of World War II that aestheticized dying in losing battles as 'honourable death', or in Japanese, '*sange*', the literal meaning of which is falling flowers. Kusunoki Masatsura and his father Masashige are well-known historical figures, especially among wartime generations, as those who were loyal to the losing southern court. They were praised in textbooks during World War II, in which Japan fought under the name of the emperor (92). Pilots of the special attack units, known as *kamikaze* pilots, often referred to them in wills they wrote before their suicidal sortie (95–96). I mentioned earlier that the title, *Ōranki*, may allude to the southern court's end, but it could also evoke *sange*.

I do not fully agree with Kawasaki, firstly because Ueda (2021: 58) stated that she aimed to dissociate Masashige and Masatsura from their wartime images to explore why they did not abandon the south from a different angle. Moreover, the home/country proposed in *Ōranki* is not like Imperial Japan as a family-state premised on the sameness of its citizens. Also, unlike Imperial Japan, the home/country would not act on capitalist logic and invade and colonize its neighbouring countries. However, like Kawasaki (2024: 119), I remain puzzled as to why Ueda chose the Kusunoki family members as the central figures of her work. This is not least because the choice she made encountered the difficulty that derives from the aestheticization of characters engaged in a military occupation on the Takarazuka stage. Battles are typically expressed through a group dance to an invigorating number; *Ōranki* is no exception. The affects that may be evoked in the audience by the overwhelming power and beauty in such scenes risk jeopardizing the critical perspectives layered into the work.

Nonetheless, if we focus on Ueda's message about the stream of care, we do find that it runs through the musical and reverberates towards the end, even

---

[59] However, this home/family can be a site for violence as Okano acknowledges, and this was evinced by a recent case of a Takarasienne's suicide due to bullying and overwork. See Postscript.

while conflicting with the aestheticized battle. When Masatsura fights his final battle, his dead father appears at the corner of the stage and sings:

> In Akasaka in Kawachi Province
> *Dokkoise dokkoise*[60]
> A camphor tree came into the bud
> With little leaves expanding
> *Aresa* it grew large
> With a root growing, leaves expanding
> If everyone gathers underneath the tree
> Earthquakes and heavy rains are not to be afraid of
> *En'yara en'yara dokkoise*
>
> (Ueda 2021: 57)

This folkloric song, composed by an in-house composer, Takahashi Megumi, to Ueda's lyrics, is sung by the Kusunoki people many times earlier with slight differences in the lyrics. The family name Kusunoki means camphor tree, so the song declares that extending care is at the heart of the Kusunokis' work. As Masatsura fights, he takes over the song from his father, and after Masatsura is fatally wounded by northern samurais' blades, it is sung by his youngest brother, Masanori (played by Tsukishiro Kanato), and the Kusunoki samurais who are also on the battlefield, suggesting that the Kusunokis' work continues in the stream of time. This is reinforced by Masatsura's dying words to Masanori: 'Don't burn down villages [in the fight with the north]. Don't let people die. No matter how long it takes, unite the country' (Ueda 2021: 57). This united country is a 'home', and it may also be a commons as an alternative to capitalism as defined by Silvia Federici and George Caffentzis: 'Commons are constituted on the basis of social cooperation, relations of reciprocity, and responsibility for the reproduction of the shared wealth, natural or produced' (Federici 2019: 95). Resonant with the notion of home conceived by Okano, it also suggests a space for '[r]espect for other people and openness to heterogeneous experiences' (95) – heterogenous also in forms of female intimacy as embodied by a 'queer' Masatsura and the queer kinship of Takarasiennes.

At the end of the musical, Masanori visits Ben no Naishi for the first time in forty years after Masatsura's death. Masanori reports on the end of the southern court, which means that unification has finally been achieved. However, the musical does not show what happens in the unified country. In contrast to *BADDY*, conflicting parties in *Ōranki* do not get together in the last scene, singing and dancing, celebrating 'heaven for all'. Instead, like the disappearing southern court, Ueda left Takarazuka a year after the production. Her last work was a big

---

[60] *Dokkoise, aresa, en'yara* in this song are calls used when body movements require effort or to enliven traditional Japanese music.

dream of an anti-capitalist, caring family, home, country, and the commons critically and crucially rendered on the capitalist stage of Takarazuka, *with the support of Takarasiennes who performed in the production*. She was cared for by them. Also, she cared for them. She almost always concluded her greetings printed in production programmes with caring comments for Takarasiennes even when they sounded out of context: 'This is the 100th year of Takarazuka. Takarasiennes have been supporting it for 100 years' (Ueda 2014: 9). 'The beauty of Takarazuka is not just in gorgeous costumes and beautiful lines [in its musicals]. Its true beauty may be in the hearts of generations of Takarasiennes' (Ueda 2015: 29). 'May Takarazuka continue to be of its students, who live hard here' (Ueda 2017: 4). Thus she demands the management's full recognition of Takarasiennes' labour, their respect and care for them. While she moved on to engagements with other theatres, on occasion she still works with some former Takarasiennes. May her bond with Takarasiennes continue; may her bond with the Takarazuka audience continue.

3.5 Concluding Reflections

The Takarazuka Revue is most hailed as an all-female company presenting boy-meets-girl romances. But this is not all that this company does. As this Element demonstrates, its productions portray various forms of non-normative love and raise political concerns despite the management's conservativism. I have analyzed female queer kinship seen through the production of *The Poe Clan*; I have also explored ways in which protests against the capitalist exploitation of women were performed by Takarasiennes in *BADDY* and *Ōranki*. Fans ardently welcomed and supported these atypical shows.

The unconventional aspects of these productions may be tamed in one sense, as what happens on the Takarazuka stage is supposed to be a 'harmless' fantasy within a girls' school. Ueda's departure may reflect her wish to enter 'reality' where her work may carry more 'weight' than in the two-dimensional fantasy world of Takarazuka. However, as explained in Section 1, fantasy works in contradictory ways in Takarazuka – to tame subversion and to imaginatively subvert reality. Fans take advantage of the former to protect the latter. Takarazuka's long history demonstrates that 'the Takarazuka clan', consisting of both Takarasiennes and fans, sustains this subversive fantasy space under the façade of 'Modesty, Fairness, Grace' – a space in which, unlike Japanese society at large, it is possible to explore and experience queer intimacy.

To the fantasy world of Takarazuka, Ueda brought real-world concerns about the exploitation of female labour, which many fans as well as Takarasiennes experience in their daily lives. The ardent support that her works received suggests that, while the fans are often thought to be apolitical, duped by 'bread and circuses', this is not always the case. They arguably utilize Takarazuka politically not only as a space of female intimacy but also as a space for inspiration and encouragement for fighting the oppression – that is, for 'activating' themselves.

As women experience the disjuncture between their material lives and the subversive fantasy world of Takarazuka, they may, like the angry Rockettes, increasingly protest the patriarchal, heteronormative constraints of Japanese society.

Postscript

This Element explored Takarazuka as a space for female intimacy; fans fantasize and adore the bond among Takarasiennes. However, the reality behind this fantasy sometimes tells a different, painful story.

On 30 September 2023, the Takarazuka community was shaken by a tragic incident. A Takarasienne from the Cosmos Troupe committed suicide due to overwork and bullying by senior Takarasiennes and staff members. The incident was widely reported by the media as part of the so-called JKT problems: J stands for Johnny & Associates, K for kabuki, and T for Takarazuka. These are all established companies or genres in Japan's entertainment industry, which has long been silencing workplace scandals.

Takarazuka fans are aware of Takarasiennes' overwork. Well before this incident, they frequently expressed concerns on social media. They are also not ignorant about bullying in this company, which promotes the bond among Takarasiennes. For example, the case of the ninety-sixth class of students at the TMS involved a court trial from 2009 to 2010 between a student, who was the target of bullying, and the school, who denied bullying.[61] The case was settled in 2010, but the details were not made public. Fans thus know that Takarazuka is not the perfect dreamland, but the suicide in 2023 shook the fan community as never before. The management admitted overwork but again denied bullying. Murakami Kōji, then the managing director and the current chairperson, declared at a press conference, 'Show us the evidence.' This arrogance and lack of sympathy towards the victim horrified the bereaved family, fans, and the wider public. Their anger at the management was rapidly circulated via social media and protests against the company surged. Some fans stopped attending shows, withdrew from the official fan club, and cancelled their contract with its cable channel (Kawai 2023). Most importantly, the bereaved family kept fighting the management. Finally, on 28 March 2024, the company issued

---

[61] The judicial complaint is printed in an issue of *Modern Theatre Studies* (*Kingendai engeki kenkyū*) (2023) with the introduction of the incident by a theatre scholar, Seto Hiroshi.

a report that, following several discussions with the family, admitted fourteen out of fifteen counts that the family listed as cases of bullying. The report also outlined the changes the company had implemented or would implement to improve workplace conditions. These include providing better counselling services and ethics training and reducing the number of annual productions and the working hours of staff members. The report also stated that the CEO of Hankyu Hanshin Holdings had apologized to the family and that compensation would be paid (Hankyu Hanshin Holdings et al. 2024). He also resigned from the board of the company and from the TMS as its president in February 2024. The Cosmos Troupe restarted performing in June 2024.

In the press conferences, what was demonstrably clear was that the executives in attendance were all male, exemplifying the masculinist ethos running through the company, men taking women's labour for granted and not showing any concern about their working conditions. Heartbreaking for fans is that such a mentality is also ingrained in some senior Takarasiennes who exploited and bullied the junior Takarasienne into accepting an excessive workload. Hence this exposed how the bond between women, much sought after and lauded by fans, does not always include all Takarasiennes. It took a human life for the brutality of the management and the seniors to be made public, and yet, sadly, although the company announced reforms, it is not clear if the seniors involved were penalized. Many fans were surprised that the company allowed them to perform when the troupe restarted in June. Even stakeholders of Hankyu Hanshin Holdings raised concerns about this in their meeting held in the same month (Tabe et al. 2024).

In January 2025, Hankyu Hanshin Holdings announced the introduction of two major changes: a reconfigured board of directors, half of whom will be from outside the Hankyu group in order to increase organizational transparency (to be implemented in July 2025), and the abolition of freelance contracts (to be implemented in March 2025). Takarasiennes who wish to continue after the first five years will be rehired on the basis of a one-year fixed-term but renewable contract, which can be converted to a permanent contract (Matsumuro & Kosaka 2025). The Hankyu group explains that this arrangement is to monitor Takarasiennes' working hours more strictly (Matsumuro & Kosaka 2025). (The Takarasienne who committed suicide was on a freelance-based contract, and freelancers' working hours are not monitored as they are supposed to work at their own discretion.) However, it is not clear if this change will radically improve Takarasiennes' working conditions. As discussed in Section 3, non-freelance Takarasiennes are also overworked despite being 'monitored'. The new system is beneficial in that it will grant all the Takarasiennes access to welfare through the company, but the fundamental problem of exploitation may remain unresolved. Another important issue is what 'roles' will be assigned to Takarasiennes on a permanent contract. Will they be able to continue performing for as long as they wish? Other questions include whether the current operation with five troupes can still work and whether Takarasiennes can marry while permanently staying in the company.

The Takarasienne's suicide may indeed jeopardize the survival of the company; in 2024, the number of applicants to the TMS was the lowest since 2000 (Asahi Shimbun 2024: 32). The company must change. Takarazuka is a safe place for female audience members to explore and experience queer intimacy, but it also must be a safe place in every sense for all the Takarasiennes.

References

Ahmed, S. (2006). *Queer Phenomenology: Orientations, Objects, Others*, Durham: Duke University Press.

Aldana Reyes, X. (2018). Dracula Queered. In R. Luckhurst, ed., *The Cambridge Companion to Dracula*, Cambridge: Cambridge University Press, pp. 125–135.

Anan, N. (2011). Two-Dimensional Imagination in Contemporary Japanese Women's Performance. *TDR: The Drama Review*, **55**(4), 96–112.

Anan, N. (2016). *Contemporary Japanese Women's Theatre and Visual Arts: Performing Girls' Aesthetics*, Basingstoke: Palgrave Macmillan.

Anan, N. (2017). Japanese Women's Popular Musicals: The Takarazuka Revue. In L. MacDonald & W. A. Everett, eds., *The Palgrave Handbook of Musical Theatre Producers*, New York: Palgrave Macmillan, pp. 145–150.

Asahi Shimbun. (2024, 28 March). Takarazuka, nyūshi kyōsōritsu 12 bai [One in Twelve Applicants Passed the Entrance Exam for Takarazuka]. *Asahi Shimbun*, Tokyo, p. 32.

Aston, E. (2020). *Restaging Feminisms*, Cham: Palgrave Macmillan.

Azuma, S. (2015). *Takarazuka, yaoi, ai no yomikae: Josei to popyurā karuchā no shakaigaku* [*Takarazuka, Yaoi, and the Replacement of Love: A Sociology of Women and Popular Culture*], Tokyo: Shin'yōsha.

Azuma, S. (2016). 2.5 jigen fan no butai no mikata: Takarazuka fan to no hikaku kara [How Fans See 2.5-Dimensional Theatre: A Comparison with Takarazuka Fans]. *Bijutsu Techō*, **68**(1038), 82–85.

Benhabib, S. (1987). The Generalized and the Concrete Other: The Kohlberg–Gilligan Controversy and Feminist Theory. In S. Benhabib & D. Cornell, eds., *Feminism as Critique: Essays on the Politics of Gender in Late-Capitalist Societies*, Minneapolis: University of Minnesota Press, pp. 77–95.

Bradway, T., & Freeman, E. (2022). Introduction: Kincoherence/Kin-aesthetics/Kinematics. In T. Bradway & E. Freeman, eds., *Queer Kinship: Race, Sex, Belonging, Form*, Durham: Duke University Press, pp. 1–22.

Case, S.-E. (1991). Tracking the Vampire. *Differences*, **3**(2), 1–20.

Daily Sports Online. (2018, 9 February). Takarazuka kagekidan 104 nen no rekishi de josei ga hatsu no shō enshutsu tsugitsugi ni odoroki no shīn [The Takarazuka Revue's 104-Year History Has Seen the First Female Directed Revue Show: One Surprising Scene after Another]. Retrieved 25 September 2024, from www.daily.co.jp/gossip/2018/02/09/0010971835.shtml.

Diamond, E. (1997). *Unmaking Mimesis: Essays on Feminism and Theater*, London: Routledge.

Dream Girls. (1994). Distributed by Women Make Movies.

EUREKA Editorial Department (ed.). (2015). Intabyū: Koyanagi Naoko 'Takarazuka' to iu sekaisen [Interview with Koyanagi Naoko: The Parallel World of 'Takarazuka']. *Eureka*, **47**(5), 127–134.

Federici, S. (2019). *Re-enchanting the World: Feminism and the Politics of the Commons*, Oakland: PM Press.

FNN Prime Online. (2023, 24 November). 'Kyūjitsu nashi' de gekkyū jū man en gekidan'in no kakoku na rōdōkankyō ga akiraka ni . . . moto sutaffu 'jibun mo karōshi rain koete ita kamo' [Monthly Salary of 100,000 Yen with No Days Off: Harsh Working Environment for the Company's Members Was Revealed. A Former Staff Member Says: 'I Might Have Come Close to Dying of Overwork']. Retrieved 20 August 2024, from www.fnn.jp/articles/-/620563.

Freeman, E. (2007). Queer Belongings: Kinship Theory and Queer Theory. In G. E. Haggerty & M. McGarry, eds., *A Companion to Lesbian, Gay, Bisexual, Transgender, and Queer Studies*, 1st ed., Malden: Blackwell, pp. 293–314.

Fujii S., & Tanaka S. (2023, 14 November). Dare ga mamoru Takarajen'nu no inochi kagekidan 'seito no ganbari ni amaeteita' [Who Protects Takarasiennes' Lives? The Company Says, 'We Have Been Depending on the Hard Work of Students']. Retrieved 2 December 2024, from www.sankei.com/article/20231114-Z6JHIRX6WVNJXE7JC7S4L2LYBE.

Gender Equality Bureau Cabinet Office. (2016). Dai 1 setsu: Subete no josei ga kagayaku shakai zukuri ni muketa seifu no ugoki [Section 1: The Government Moves towards Creating a Society Where Every Woman Shines]. Retrieved 19 August 2024, from www.gender.go.jp/about_danjo/whitepaper/h27/zentai/html/honpen/b1_s00_01.html.

Hagio, M. (1998). *Pō no ichizoku* [*The Poe Clan*], Vol. 1, Tokyo: Shogakukan.

Hankyu Hanshin Holdings. (2010). *Anyuaru ripōto* [*Annual Report*] 2010. www.hankyu-hanshin.co.jp/upload/irRelatedInfo/16.pdf.

Hankyu Hanshin Holdings. (2023). *Tōgōhōkokusho* [*Integrated Report*] 2022. www.hankyu-hanshin.co.jp/docs/integratedreport2022_j_print.pdf.

Hankyu Hanshin Holdings, Hankyu Railway, & The Takarazuka Revue. (2024, 28 March). Takarazuka kagekidan soragumi gekidan'in no seikyo ni kansuru goizoku tono gōisho teiketsu no gohōkoku narabi ni saihatsu bōshi ni muketa torikumi ni tsuite [Report on the Conclusion of an Agreement with the Bereaved Family of the Takarazuka Revue Company's Cosmos Troupe Member Who Died and Actions Taken to Prevent a Recurrence]. Retrieved 13 November 2024 from https://kageki.hankyu.co.jp/news/pdf/20240328_003.pdf.

Iizuka, T. (2022). Ongaku ni kakawari tsuzukete mieta koto: Ueda Kumiko [Ueda Kumiko: What I Was Able to See as I Continued Working with Music]. *Higeki Kigeki* [*Tragedy, Comedy*], **75**(4), 11–17.

Itō, A. (2022). Atarashī 'higeki' o tsumugu hito: Ueda Kumiko Ōranki ga toikakeru mono [A Director Who Creates A New 'Tragedy': Ueda Kumiko's Exploration through Ōranki]. *Butai Geijutsu* [*Performing Arts*], **25**, 130–138.

Iwamoto, T. (2020). Takarazuka no kishu: Koike Shūichirō to iu enshutsuka [A Standard-Bearer of Takarazuka: Director Koike Shūichirō]. In *Takarazukaizumu* [*Takarazuka-ism*], **41**, Tokyo: Seikyūsha, pp. 54–57.

Iwashita, H. (2020). *Kyara ga riaru ni naru toki: 2 jigen, 2.5 jigen, sonosaki no kyarakutā ron* [*When Characters Become Real: A Theory of Characters That Are 2D, 2.5D, and Beyond*], Tokyo: Seidosha.

Kakinuma, E. (2007). Anne Rice no Vanpaiazō [Images of Vampires in Anne Rice's Work]. *Yasō*, 54–60.

Katada, K. (2021). *Ikiru tame no feminizumu: Pan to bara to shihonshugi* [*Feminism to Live: Bread, Roses, and Capitalism*], Tokyo: Taba Books.

Katō, A. (2019). Ai to yūgasa de tsukuri ageta chōtairin no hana [Ultra-Large Flower Made of Love and Grace]. *Takarazukaizumu* [*Takarazuka-ism*], **40**, 17–20.

Kawai, M. (2023, 12 June). Takarazuka kagekidan 'kawatte hoshī' kunō no fan, chiketto kyanseru mo [Anguished Fans Who 'Want Change' at the Takarazuka Revue Cancel Their Tickets]. *Asahi Digital*. Retrieved 13 November 2024 from www.asahi.com/articles/ASRCZ3279RCVUCVL010.html.

Kawasaki, K. (1999). *Takarazuka: Shōhi shakai no supekutakuru* [*Takarazuka: Spectacles of a Consumer Society*], Tokyo: Kōdansha.

Kawasaki, K. (2005). *Takarazuka to iu yūtopia* [*A Utopia Called Takarazuka*], Tokyo: Iwanami shoten.

Kawasaki, K. (2022). *Takarazuka: Henyō o tsuzukeru 'Nihon modanizumu'* [*Takarazuka: A Continually Transforming 'Japanese Modernism'*], Tokyo: Iwanami shoten.

Kawasaki, K. (2024). Takarazuka ni okeru 'inochi' no hyōgen: Shibata Yukihiro, Masatsuka Haruhiko kara Ueda Kumiko made [Depictions of 'Life' in Takarazuka: Shibata Yukihiro, Masatsuka Haruhiko, and Ueda Kumiko]. *Bungaku Geijutsu* [*Arts and Letters*], **45**, 85–119.

Kiyono, Y. (2023). Gendai no shōzō enshutsuka Ueda Kumiko [Portraits of the Present: Director Ueda Kumiko]. *AERA*, **36**(4), 48–53.

Koike, S. (1998). Banpanera no fūin [The Seal of Vampires]. In *Pō no ichizoku* [*The Poe Clan*], Vol. 1, Tokyo: Shogakukan, pp. 296–300.

Koike, S. (2018a). Kami wa fūin o tokareta [The God Broke the Seal]. In *Takarazuka: Pō no ichizoku* [*The Poe Clan*], p. 5.

Koike, S. (2018b). *Pō no ichizoku* [*The Poe Clan*]. *Le CINQ*, **189**, 45–67.

Koike, S. (2021). Special Interview: Koike Shūichirō [*The Poe Clan*: Special Disc].

Kotake, S. (2005). Gansaku Takarazuka rekishikan: Takarazuka ni okeru shōnen-ai no rekishi [A Forged History of Takarazuka: A History of *Shōnen-ai* in Takarazuka]. *Takarazuka Akademia* [*Takarazuka Academy*], **23**, 196–199.

Kurahashi, S., & Tsuji, N. (2005). *Shōjo kageki no kōbō: Hitotoki no yume no ato* [*A Glimmer of Girls' Opera: Traces of a Brief Dream*], Tokyo: Seikyūsha.

MacDonald, L. (2023). 'A New Path to the Future': Woman Producers of Border-Crossing Musical Theatre in Japan, South Korea, and China. *Theatre Topics*, **33**(2), 65–81.

Mainichi Shimbun. (2023, 10 July). Takarazuka kageki de saien 'Berusaiyu no bara' to wa 74nen shoen, ichidai būmu ni [The Takarazuka Revue's Revival of *The Rose of Versailles*: First Performed in 1974, It Became a Huge Hit]. Retrieved 6 May 2024, from https://mainichi.jp/articles/20230710/k00/00m/200/212000c.

Matsumuro, H. (2024, 3 July). Hikari to yami: Takarazuka gekidan'in shibō danketsu habanda tarento sei 77nen dōnyū koyōkeiyaku ippen [Light and Darkness: Death of a Takarazuka Member. The Freelance System Introduced in 1977 Hindered Solidarity as It Completely Changed the Employment Contracts]. *Mainichi Shimbun*, Tokyo, p. 1.

Matsumuro, H., & Kosaka, T. (2025, 15 January). Takarazuka, koyō kakudai 6nen-me ikō mo kabushikigaishaka [Takarazuka Becomes a Corporation and Expands Employment Contracts for 6th-Year or Older Takarasiennes]. *Mainichi Shimbun*, p. 19.

Matsumuro, H., & Seki, Y. (2023, 15 November). Kurōzuappu: Takarazuka, igi hasamenu heisasei gekidan'in kyūshi chōsahōkoku tsuyoi kōsoku, dokuji na keiyaku [Close-Up: Closed Nature of Takarazuka That Excludes Objections. Sudden Death of a Member. Report of an Investigation. Strong Constraints. Unfair Contracts]. *Mainichi Shimbun*, p. 3.

McRobbie, A. (2016). *Be Creative: Making a Living in the New Culture Industries*, Cambridge: Polity Press.

Miyabe, M. (1998). *Pō no ichizoku* ni tsuite [About *The Poe Clan*]. In *Pō no ichizoku* [*The Poe Clan*], Vol. 2, Tokyo: Shogakukan, pp. 298–301.

Miyamoto, K. (2019). Hanagumi no idai na toppusutā ni ai to kansha o komete [To the Great Top Star of the Flower Troupe, with Love and Gratitude]. *Takarazukaizumu* [*Takarazuka-ism*], **40**, 21–24.

Miyawaki, R., & Okabayashi, S. (2024, 10 May). First Proper Look at Wage Gap between the Sexes across Japan. Retrieved 17 December 2024 from Asahi Shimbum. www.asahi.com/ajw/articles/15415546.

Nakamoto, C. (2011). *Naze Takarazuka no otokoyaku wa kakkoīnoka: Kankyaku o miryō suru 'otokoyaku' wa kōshite tsukurareru* [*Why Are Takarazuka's Male-Role Players Cool?: How to Create 'Male-Role Players' Who Mesmerize the Audience*], Tokyo: Tokyodo shuppan.

Nanashima, S. (2023). *Takarazuka no zatsukisakka o osu!: Sutā o sasaeru tateyakusha tachi* [*Pushing In-House Directors in Takarazuka!: Leading Players Supporting the Stars*], Tokyo: Seikyūsha.

National Tax Agency. (2024). Reiwa 5 nenbun minkan kyūyo jittai tōkei chōsa [National Survey of Private Sector Salaries 2023]. Retrieved 2 December 2024, from www.nta.go.jp/publication/statistics/kokuzeicho/minkan/gaiyou/2023.htm.

Okano, Y. (2012). *Feminizumu no seijigaku: Kea no rinri o gurōbaru shakai e* [*Feminist Politics: Ethics of Care in a Global Society*], Tokyo: Mizu shobō.

Rich, A. (1980). Compulsory Heterosexuality and Lesbian Existence. *Signs*, **5**(4), 631–660.

Rich, A. (1986). *Blood, Bread, and Poetry: Selected Prose 1979–1985*, New York: W. W. Norton & Company.

Rich, A. (2004). Reflections on 'Compulsory Heterosexuality'. *Journal of Women's History*, **16**(1), 9–11.

Robertson, J. E. (1998). *Takarazuka: Sexual Politics and Popular Culture in Modern Japan*, Berkeley: University of California Press.

Sakabe, Y. (2020). Dēta de miru Takarajen'nu: 'Zaidankikan' to 'taidan' ni tsuite no shūkei [Takarasiennes in Data: Aggregation of Tenure and Retirement]. *Journal of the Japan Society for Digital Archive*, **4**(2), 199–202.

Satō, S. (2007). Eien to iu kurushimi [Suffering from Eternity]. *Yasō*, 20–31.

Seto, H. (2023). Takarazuka ongaku gakkō 96-ki saiban sojō kaidai [Trial Complaint: The Trial Involved with the Class of Ninety-Sixth at the Takarazuka Music School]. *Kingendai Engeki Kenkyū* [*Modern Theatre Studies*], **11**, 44–63.

Shamoon, D. M. (2012). *Passionate Friendship: The Aesthetics of Girls' Culture in Japan*, Honolulu: University of Hawaii Press.

Stickland, L. R. (2008). *Gender Gymnastics: Performing and Consuming Japan's Takarazuka Revue*, Melbourne: Trans Pacific.

Sugawa, A. (2021). *2.5jigen butairon: butai, kyarakutā, fandamu* [*Theorizing 2.5-dimensional Culture: Stage, Characters, and Fandom*], Tokyo: Seikyūsha.

Tabe, A., Doi, E., & Kawai, M. (2024, 18 June). Takarazuka soragumi, kōen saikai e 'hitsuyō na taiō aimai na mama' shiteki mo [Takarazuka's Cosmos

Troupe to Restart Performances: 'Necessary Actions Remain Unclear,' Some Point Out]. *Asahi Digital*. Retrieved 13 November 2024 from www.asahi.com/articles/ASS6K2QTTS6KUCVL00RM.html.

Tabe, A., & Kawai, M. (2024, 18 February). Purodhūsā josei zero tuzuku jittai [The Lack of Female Producers Continues to Be a Reality]. *Asahi Shimbun*, Tokyo, p. 26.

Takarazuka Music School. (n.d.). Butaijin ni naru! Takarajen'nu ga umareru tokoro [Becoming Performers! – Where Takarasiennes Are Born]. Retrieved 30 November 2024 from www.tms.ac.jp/images/school_info.pdf.

Tamai, H. (1999). *Takarazuka ni saita seishun* [*The Blooming Youth in Takarazuka*], Tokyo: Seikyūsha.

Tamaki, Y. (2011). Jikkenteki kōen: *Nijinsky* to iu chōsen [Experimental Production: *Nijinsky*'s Challenge]. *Takarazukaizumu* [*Takarazuka-ism*], **17**, 71–74.

The Takarazuka Revue. (2022). Gakkō kangekikai no goan'nai [Students' Attendance to Takarazuka Shows]. Retrieved 21 October 2024 from https://kageki.hankyu.co.jp/sp/cpl73a00000c4qs6-att/cpl73a00000c4u2e.pdf.

Thompson, J. (2020). Towards an Aesthetics of Care. In A. Stuart Fisher & J. Thompson, eds., *Performing Care: New Perspectives on Socially Engaged Performance*, Manchester: Manchester University Press, pp. 36–48.

Tsuji, N. (2004). *Otoko tachi no Takarazuka: Yume o otta kenkyūsei no hanseiki* [*Men's Takarazuka: Half a Century of Students Who Pursued Their Dreams*], Kobe: Kobe Shimbun sōgō shuppan sentā.

Tsuruoka, E. (2018). Takarazuka ni jiritsu shita musumeyaku no kanōsei o hiraita keu na sonzai, Manaki Reika ni yosete [To Manaki Reika, a Pioneering Independent Female-Role Player in Takarazuka]. *Takarazukaizumu* [*Takarazuka-ism*], **37**, 8–9.

Ubukata, T. (2009). Ai o tsugeru mono: Hagio Moto no sakuhin ni okeru 'kagami' no kinō [One Who Conveys Love: Functions of 'Mirror' in Hagio Moto's Work]. In Y. Iida, T. Shimamura, O. Takahashi, & A. Nakayama, eds., *Shōjo shōnen no poritikusu* [*The Politics of Girls and Boys*], Tokyo: Seidosha, pp. 240–256.

Uchino, T. (2009). *Crucible Bodies: Postwar Japanese Performance from Brecht to the New Millennium*, London: Seagull Books.

Ueda, K. (2014). *Tsubasa aru hitobito*. In *TAKARAZUKA: Tsubasa aru hitobito: Burāmusu to Kurara Shūman* [*People with Wings: Brahms and Clara Schumann*], p. 9.

Ueda, K. (2015). *Hoshiai hitoyo*. In *TAKARAZUKA: Hoshiai hitoyo* [*One Night of Stars*] *and La Esmeralda*, p. 29.

Ueda, K. (2017). *Kamigami no tochi*. In *TAKARAZUKA: Kamigami no tochi: Romanofu tachi no tasogare* [*The Land of the Gods: The Twilight of the Romanovs*] *and Kurashikaru bijū* [*Classical Bijoux*], p. 4.

Ueda, K. (2018a). *BADDY*. In *TAKARAZUKA: Kanpanī: doryoku, jōnetsu, soshite nakamatachi* [*Company: Lessons, Passion, and Companionship*] *and BADDY: yatsu wa tsuki kara yattekuru* [*BADDY: A Rogue from the Moon*], p. 5.

Ueda, K. (2018b). Booklet of CD: *BADDY: Yatsu wa tsuki kara yattekuru* [*BADDY: A Rogue from the Moon*]. CD: *BADDY: Yatsu wa tsuki kara yattekuru* [*BADDY: A Rogue from the Moon*].

Ueda, K. (2018c). Pan to sākasu no abunai jidai ni [In a Dangerous Time of Bread and Circuses]. In *Pan to sākasu no abunai jidai ni* [*In a Dangerous Time of Bread and Circuses*], Yoshida Campus, Kyoto University, pp. 1–25.

Ueda, K. (2021). *Ōranki*. Le CINQ, **215**, 45–59.

Ueda, K., & Members of the Moon Troupe. (2018). Zadankai *BADDY: Yatsu wa tsuki kara yattekuru* [Round-table Talk: *BADDY: A Rogue from the Moon*]. *Kageki* [*Opera*], **1109**, 74–81.

Ueda, K., & Members of the Moon Troupe. (2021). Zadankai *Ōranki* [Round-table Talk: *Ōranki*]. *Kageki* [*Opera*], **1148**, 56–65.

Umehara, R., & Otohara, A. (1994). *Takarazuka for Beginners*, Tokyo: Gendai shokan.

Wolf, S. (2002). *A Problem Like Maria: Gender and Sexuality in the American Musical*, Ann Arbor: University of Michigan Press.

Yabushita, T. (2019). Otokoyaku no rekishi ni aratana 1pēji o kakikuwaeta keu na sutā [A Rare Star Who Added a New Page to the History of Male-Role Players]. *Takarazukaizumu* [*Takarazuka-ism*], **40**, 7–9.

Yamanashi, M. (2012). *A History of the Takarazuka Revue since 1914: Modernity, Girls' Culture, Japan Pop*, Leiden: Global Oriental.

Yamanashi, M. (2023). *Performing Cross-Cultural Modernity: Behind and Beyond Japan's Takarazuka Revue*. Osaka: Union Press.

York, E. (2021). Eden in Sin City: Adapting for the Musical Theater Body in Takarazuka Revue's *Ocean's 11*. *Dance Chronicle*, **44**(2), 151–181.

Yoshida, J. (2023, 26 January). Takarazuka no ryūgi, opera bunka ni idomu motozatsuki Ueda Kumiko, hatsu no enshutsu [Takarazuka Style and A Challenge to the Opera Culture: Former In-House Director Ueda Kumiko's First Directions]. *Asahi Shimbun*, p. 3.

Acknowledgements

I would like to thank Elaine Aston for inviting me to write this Element about Takarazuka. My first monograph was also in the series she edited. My scholarly development is indebted to the support and opportunities she generously provided me.

My heartfelt thanks also go to my mentors, Carol Fisher Sorgenfrei, Sue-Ellen Case and Janelle Reinelt. My work on Takarazuka started in my final paper for Sue-Ellen's course on identity and identification at the University of California, Los Angeles and was further developed in my PhD dissertation on Japanese women's performance with Carol as my advisor. Parts of it were refined and included in my first monograph that I started to write under the mentorship of Janelle as her postdoc at the University of Warwick.

A shorter version of Section 2 of this Element was presented at the Feminist Theatre Working Group at the meeting of the International Federation for Theatre Research in Manila in 2024. I am grateful for the comments and insights that the members shared with me on the manuscript. I also thank my colleague and friend Azuma Sonoko. Her excellent work on Takarazuka and our discussion about the company have always been a source of inspiration.

My deepest thanks go to my husband, who is always my first reader. He was there next to me as I wrote this Element, as he has been over all these years. In fact, he is right here now, checking how I thank him in my acknowledgements.

Cambridge Elements⁼

Women Theatre Makers

Elaine Aston
Lancaster University

Elaine Aston is internationally acclaimed for her feminism and theatre research. Her monographs include *Caryl Churchill* (1997); *Feminism and Theatre* (1995); *Feminist Theatre Practice* (1999); *Feminist Views on the English Stage* (2003); and *Restaging Feminisms* (2020). She has served as Senior Editor of Theatre Research International (2010–12) and President of the International Federation for Theatre Research (2019–23).

Melissa Sihra
Trinity College Dublin

Melissa Sihra is Associate Professor in Drama and Theatre Studies at Trinity College Dublin. She is author of *Marina Carr: Pastures of the Unknown* (2018) and editor of *Women in Irish Drama: A Century of Authorship and Representation* (2007). She was President of the Irish Society for Theatre Research (2011–15) and is currently researching a feminist historiography of the Irish playwright and co-founder of the Abbey Theatre, Lady Augusta Gregory.

Advisory Board

Nobuko Anan, *Kansai University, Japan*
Awo Mana Asiedu, *University of Ghana*
Ana Bernstein, *UNIRIO, Brazil*
Elin Diamond, *Rutgers, USA*
Bishnupriya Dutt, *JNU, India*
Penny Farfan, *University of Calgary, Canada*
Lesley Ferris, *Ohio State University, USA*
Lisa FitzPatrick, *University of Ulster, Northern Ireland*
Lynette Goddard, *Royal Holloway, University of London, UK*
Sarah Gorman, *Roehampton University, UK*
Aoife Monks, *Queen Mary, London University, UK*
Kim Solga, *Western University, Canada*
Denise Varney, *University of Melbourne, Australia*

About the Series

This innovative, inclusive series showcases women-identifying theatre makers from around the world. Expansive in chronological and geographical scope, the series encompasses practitioners from the late nineteenth century onwards and addresses a global, comprehensive range of creatives – from playwrights and performers to directors and designers.

Cambridge Elements

Women Theatre Makers

Elements in the Series

Maya Rao and Indian Feminist Theatre
Bishnupriya Dutt

Xin Fengxia and the Transformation of China's Ping Opera
Siyuan Liu

Emma Rice's Feminist Acts of Love
Lisa Peck

Women Making Shakespeare in the Twenty-First Century
Kim Solga

Clean Break Theatre Company
Caoimhe McAvinchey, Sarah Bartley, Deborah Dean and Anne-marie Greene

#WakingTheFeminists and the Data-Driven Revolution in Irish Theatre
Claire Keogh

The Theatre of Louise Lowe
Miriam Haughton

Ellen Terry, Shakespeare, and Suffrage in Australia and New Zealand
Kate Flaherty

Performing Female Intimacy in Japan's Takarazuka Revue
Nobuko Anan

A full series listing is available at: www.cambridge.org/EWTM

For EU product safety concerns, contact us at Calle de José Abascal, 56–1º,
28003 Madrid, Spain or eugpsr@cambridge.org.

www.ingramcontent.com/pod-product-compliance
Lightning Source LLC
LaVergne TN
LVHW011858060526
838200LV00054B/4401